THAI in 7

THAI in 7

DELICIOUS THAI RECIPES IN 7 INGREDIENTS OR FEWER

SEBBY HOLMES

PHOTOGRAPHY BY NASSIMA ROTHACKER

KYLE BOOKS

An Hachette UK Company
www.hachette.co.uk

First published in Great Britain in 2020 by
Kyle Books, an imprint of Kyle Cathie Ltd
Carmelite House
50 Victoria Embankment
London EC4Y 0DZ
www.kylebooks.co.uk

ISBN: 978 085783 834 6

Distributed in the US by Hachette Book Group,
1290 Avenue of the Americas, 4th and 5th Floors,
New York, NY 10104

Distributed in Canada by Canadian Manda Group,
664 Annette St., Toronto, Ontario, Canada M6S 2C8

Publisher: Joanna Copestick
Editorial director: Judith Hannam
Editor: Vicky Orchard
Editorial assistant: Sarah Kyle
Design: Georgia Vaux
Photography: Nassima Rothacker
Food styling: Becks Wilkinson
Props styling: Morag Farquhar
Production: Gemma John and Nic Jones

A Cataloguing in Publication record for this title is available
from the British Library

Printed and bound in China

10 9 8 7 6 5 4 3 2 1

CONTENTS

INTRODUCTION

Food has always been an integral part of my life. My nan used to hide extra scrambled eggs under my toast in the morning as I was so excited by the prospect of extending my breakfast a little bit longer, which probably explains my growing waistline, too!

I have worked in professional kitchens since I was thirteen and had my hands on a pan ever since. I still remember walking into my first kitchen in London, at a restaurant called The Begging Bowl in Peckham. It was here that I was introduced to Thai cuisine, which led me to devoting my career to it, opening a Thai restaurant and writing this book. After three years behind the wok there, I was offered my first Head Chef role at a new restaurant called The Smoking Goat focused around Thai barbecue. As soon as the doors opened, this little restaurant just got busier and busier and after a year I decided to open my own restaurant: Farang. This started as a street food concept, setting up kitchens for the day or weekend at food markets and events. These were interesting times as we were cooking for the ambassador of Thailand one day and the American Embassy the next. After a few years, I was offered the opportunity to take over the lease of my own restaurant in Highbury as my stepfather was retiring, leaving his old Italian trattoria up for grabs. Without a penny to my name, I made the call to give my own restaurant a crack – a decision that at the time seemed a little mad and, to be honest, still does, but we have been open for just shy of three years and have held a Michelin Bib Gourmand for two. An English chef cooking Thai food from an Italian restaurant in London – hopefully this paints a suitable image of the the weird, wonderful, exciting and, quite frankly, random world in which my cooking career has flourished.

I was trained from a youngster to follow the seasons when sourcing ingredients. This lesson has stuck with me and I truly feel that using ingredients that are in season and at their best is the only way to cook. Farang does just that. We source and forage the best-quality ingredients that we can get our hands on in the UK and across Thailand. Due to my English heritage, I have never focused my cooking on complete authenticity as that is an almost impossible task outside Thailand, but instead I devote myself to flavour and taste. I even named my restaurant Farang, which translates as "white foreigner" in Thai, to emphasise my naturally non-authentic cooking style. This allows for a little more playfulness when it comes to creating recipes. It is important for me to learn and understand the origins of a dish, why and how it exists, what it should taste like and how it should be cooked. From there, the necessary fundamentals are kept but a few changes may be made to make it more suitable for cooking outside Thailand, using only ingredients that are readily available.

Thai cuisine fascinates me, there really is nothing else quite like it. Its complex mixture of sweet, salty, sour, spicy and bitter flavours means that I can happily cook and eat it every day. Thai food culture is based around sharing and eating together and dishes are intensely seasoned as they are served with rice and shared amongst friends and family. Lots of Farang's customers share my passion for Thai cuisine but find it difficult to discover accessible recipes that are possible to cook outside Thailand, or if you do not have access to some of the rarer ingredients. In *Thai in 7*, I wanted to make everyone feel comfortable enough to pick up a pestle and mortar and have a crack at cooking Thai food themselves, without the restraints of difficult ingredient sourcing. All these recipes use accessible ingredients, and if a rarer ingredient is used traditionally, I mention this so you can go on the hunt for it if you like.

If you have cooked Thai food, you will probably know that many recipes can use 15–30 ingredients.

Dishes are built from layers of subtle flavours being carefully incorporated. A classic Thai green curry starts with combining about 15 ingredients in a pestle and mortar, a lengthy process that takes a lot of muscle. This is fried out, seasoned and coconut cream, stock, meat or vegetables and herbs added – using about 30 ingredients in total and taking the best part of a few hours. My aim in this book is to provide you with recipes that are not as complex and time-consuming as these traditional versions. You will notice that there are a few curry recipes, however, I have steered clear of any complex curries as it is just not possible to make flavourful pastes using only a handful of ingredients.

If you want to regularly cook Thai food there are a few essential condiments and ingredients that you will need for almost every recipe. You should have these in your cupboards or fridge at all times, as you would salt and pepper. I have used these "cheats" as basic ingredients that are not counted as part of the seven and are highlighted in the method of the recipes. These are:

Fish sauce – A liquid condiment made from fermented fish and water, this is intensely salty and fishy, yet savoury and umami. Once opened, it should be kept refrigerated and will keep indefinitely, so is easy to stock at home. A common misconception is that fish sauce should be kept out of the fridge, but this causes it to oxidise faster, darkening in colour and intensifying in flavour. To test fish sauce, hold it up to the light; it should be golden brown and you should be able to see light through it. Many people swap soy sauce for fish sauce and although very different in flavour, it is essentially a meat-free, liquid salt alternative, so it is a convenient replacement. However, there are more similar alternatives available. You can now buy seaweed sauce, a liquid-based salt solution made from fermented seaweed. This imparts a flavour of the sea in the same way that fish sauce does, so it's a much more suitable meat-free option. There are also brands of gluten-free soy sauce available, so whatever your dietary requirements, there is something for you. Recipes are flagged as gluten-free, vegetarian and vegan where applicable.

Vegetable oil – Traditionally coconut oil is used across Thailand, specifically when cooking curries and stir-fries. However, to keep things simpler and more affordable, I've used vegetable oil for most recipes.

Chillies – Chillies are used as a seasoning in Thai food, not just to add spice but to bring sweetness, bitterness, colour and vibrancy. To remove the chillies from a recipe is like taking out the salt, it will affect the overall balance and flavour of the dish. Throughout the book, fresh long green, long red and dried long red chillies are used alongside green and red bird's eye chillies, each chilli imparting its own characteristics. In some recipes, the colour of the chilli is not important so either can be used. Generally, the smaller the chilli, the spicier it will be. Green chillies tend to be spicy and bitter, while red ones have ripened to a sweeter flavour. In the industry, we call bird's eye chillies "scuds", aptly named after the World War II tactical missiles because if you are not careful then they can pack a serious punch. Both long and bird's eye chillies are readily available in most supermarkets and feature in many recipes, so keep these stocked in your fridge. At home I grow my own chillies as I find that they always do well sat on the window ledge.

Garlic – Garlic is fundamental to Thai cooking; it has been a common seasoning for thousands of years and appears frequently in my recipes, so it is another essential "cheat".

There are a few "hero" ingredients in Thai cuisine that appear in many dishes. These ingredients might have been slightly difficult to find a few years ago, but with the growing popularity of Asian cuisine they can now be picked up at most large supermarkets.

Galangal – Galangal is a rhizome and, like ginger, it is woody in texture and spicy, intense and fragrant in flavour. You can get hold of it in most large supermarkets, but it can be purchased online or ginger used as replacement.

Palm sugar – Good-quality palm sugar is soft to the touch, almost toffee-like in consistency and is traditionally used in most Thai dishes that require sweetness. It can be purchased in solid blocks from most supermarkets and while it is usually not quite as good in quality as palm sugar in Thailand, it is good enough. Its best characteristic is its subtle sweetness, so it does not overwhelm a dish but heightens the overall flavour. If you struggle to find palm sugar, light soft brown sugar is a good alternative.

Coconut cream – I have found that the best coconut cream you can buy tends to be anything packaged in cardboard, rather than in a can. The can taints the flavour, taking away from its naturally delicious sweetness. If you can only find cans, have a look at the ingredients and try to buy one that contains over 80% coconut – you will be amazed at how little coconut is in some cans.

Lemongrass – Lemongrass is a little trickier to find in most supermarkets but its sweet, citrus aroma and flavour is vital to many Thai dishes, so you will see it pop up throughout my recipes. In most cases it is only the young, softer lemongrass that you need for cooking. Due to how long it has travelled to get to the shop shelf, most lemongrass tends to have a tougher, woodier outer layer that should be removed to gain access to the softer, more fragrant and edible interior. However, the outer layer can be thrown into stocks, soups or stews for extra flavour..

Kaffir lime leaves – Similarly to lemongrass these leaves can get expensive when buying them fresh as they are normally sold in small amounts in most supermarkets. Your best bet is to buy them frozen from an Asian supermarket and use as and when you need them.

Limes – Limes are commonly used in my recipes. Sometimes the sourness of fresh lime is part of the dish itself, or used in a dressing or marinade and in others a cheek or wedge of lime is served with the finished dish to add sharp hit.

Tamarind – Tamarind is a pod-like fruit that contains a sour pulp. It is most commonly sold in blocks to which you add a little water and then strain it to remove the flavour of the tamarind without any of the seeds or pulp. Tamarind is sour in flavour with a natural sweetness and a thick, brown consistency and colour. It is mostly used in soups, stir-fries and dressings.

Noodles – I only use noodles that are readily available in most supermarkets. Although fresh noodles are best, you may not find them very easily. Dried rice, egg and glass noodles are still delicious and much cheaper and widely available. Some need to be blanched in salted water until soft and others soaked in cold water and then stir-fried until completely cooked. Follow the packet instructions if you are in doubt.

Rice – Rice is fundamental to Thai cuisine and most dishes in this book are designed to be eaten with rice. I have used the two most common forms of Thai rice – jasmine rice and sticky rice – so you should always be able to get you hands on them with ease. However, be aware that you will need a rice steamer to make sticky rice.

In terms of equipment the only bit of kit that you need to cook Thai food is a pestle and mortar. These come in different shapes and materials, but I suggest getting a medium, granite pestle and mortar. When making pastes and dressings using a pestle and mortar, combining ingredients using brute force fuses the flavours and textures in a way that cannot be replicated using a blender or a food processor. Be careful not to break the pestle on the floor otherwise legend has it that it's seven years bad luck.

SNACKS, SIDES & SALADS

SOY & WHITE PEPPER CHICKEN CRISPS

These days, we are all aware of the global impact of food waste and it is our duty to try our hardest to minimize it. We put this dish on at the restaurant, as we were shredding lots of chicken for a particular dish and were left with all the skin. Skin is a little too fatty to be used in stocks, so we marinated it and turned it into crisps.

Makes a perfect snack for 2. Gluten-free (use gluten-free soy sauce and cornflour)

about 80g (2¾oz) chicken skin	2 tablespoons light soy sauce	2 teaspoons caster sugar	small pinch of ground white pepper	6 tablespoons cornflour (or plain flour)

You can make these either by deep-frying or by roasting – frying is faster but roasting is tastiest (both are delicious). Roughly chop the chicken skin into 5cm (2in) squares.

To make the marinade, using a pestle and mortar, pound together **2 peeled garlic cloves** and **1 red or green bird's eye chilli** to make a paste, using a little coarse salt as an abrasive, then add the soy sauce and caster sugar (or blend together in a food processor). Place the chicken skin pieces in a mixing bowl, add the marinade and coat thoroughly. Cover and either leave to marinate for a few hours in the fridge or for 30 minutes at room temperature (chicken skin doesn't take long to take on flavour as it is thin and porous).

For the roasted chicken skin crisps, preheat the oven to 180°C/350°F/gas mark 4.

Lay the chicken skin over a rack placed in a grill pan or baking tin, discarding any excess marinade. Roast for 25–30 minutes until the skin is golden brown and crispy. Remove from the oven, lightly dust with the white pepper and then cool for a few minutes before serving – the skin will crisp up even more once it has cooled a little.

For the fried chicken skin crisps, combine the cornflour (or flour) and white pepper in a mixing bowl, then add the marinated chicken skin pieces and toss them in the cornflour/flour mixture using your hands until thoroughly coated all over. Heat **800ml (28fl oz) vegetable oil** in a deep, heavy-based pan over a medium heat to around 180°C (350°F). To check the temperature, place a piece of chicken skin into the hot oil and see how it reacts – if it bubbles gently and floats on the surface, this is perfect.

Deep-fry the marinated skins, 4–5 pieces at a time, for about 1 minute on each side until golden brown. Remove from the oil using a slotted spoon and drain on kitchen paper. Repeat with the remaining chicken skins. Cool a little and then enjoy. Both versions are delicious served on their own or with a dipping sauce, such as the Tomato, Chilli & Tamarind Barbecue Sauce (see page 139).

CHILLI MANGO SALAD

Sweet, salty, spicy and sour, this dish takes its flavour profile to the maximum. A great little tip to add texture to the salad is to finely slice some dried mango and garnish the salad with it. The jerk-like consistency in the mouth adds a tasty touch to this already banging salad.

Feeds 2. Vegetarian, vegan, gluten-free (use seaweed sauce or gluten-free soy sauce, if you like)

3 teaspoons caster sugar	juice of 3 limes	juice of 1 clementine	3 tablespoons light soy sauce	small handful of mint leaves, torn	small handful of coriander leaves, stems removed	1 ripe mango, peeled, stoned and sliced into bite-sized chunks

Start by preparing the "nahm yum" dressing. Using a pestle and mortar, pound together **2 peeled garlic cloves** and **3 chopped long green chillies** into a coarse paste, using the caster sugar as an abrasive. Stir in the lime juice, clementine juice and soy sauce, then taste. The dressing should taste sweet, salty, spicy and sour in equal measure, so adjust the taste as required.

Next, place the mint, coriander and prepared mango in a mixing bowl with a few tablespoons of the dressing and toss well to combine all the flavours. Pour the remaining dressing on to a serving dish, then place the salad on top. It is important not to overdress the salad as you still want to taste all the individual ingredients.

Serve the salad with steamed jasmine rice to mop up all the dressing.

STICKY PALM SUGAR & FISH SAUCE CHICKEN WINGS

Fish sauce wings, the cornerstone of Thai snack food and a dish that is relatively simple to pull off. I first tried these from a street food vender on Khoasan Road in Bangkok – she had a large wok filled with oil on one side of her stand and another wok over burning charcoal on the other side, fully loaded to smash out some serious chicken wings to the masses. My version is a little simpler today and does not involve quite as many woks, but the taste is banging.

Feeds 2. Gluten-free

6 large chicken wings, roughly 400g (14oz), excess skin and fat trimmed off	300g (10½oz) rice flour, plus an extra tablespoon	80g (2¾oz) palm sugar (or 50g/1¾oz caster sugar)	2 tablespoons tamarind paste	a shot of whisky (optional)	a few mint leaves, torn up a little	a few coriander leaves

First, marinate the chicken wings. Pound **50ml (2fl oz) of fish sauce** and **8 peeled garlic cloves** to a paste using a pestle and mortar, or finely chop the garlic and combine with the fish sauce in a bowl. Add the chicken wings and mix thoroughly to coat, then cover and leave to marinate, ideally overnight in the fridge or for at least for 2 hours.

Next, fry the wings. Heat **1 litre (1¾ pints) of vegetable oil** in a deep, heavy-based pan over a medium heat to around 160°C (325°F). Check the temperature by putting a little chicken skin (from trimming the wings) in the hot oil, it should bubble gently and float on the surface when the oil is hot enough.

Meanwhile, place the rice flour in a large tray and coat the marinated chicken wings in the flour (don't worry if you scoop a little of the minced garlic up, too, this will cook as you fry the wings and add to the deliciousness). Set the leftover marinade to one side to use in the glaze.

Deep-fry the chicken wings in batches of three for 10–12 minutes until they are cooked through, turning them in the oil every minute or so. To check the wings are cooked, use a meat thermometer (the internal temperature should be at least 78°C/172°F) or cut the largest one down to the bone and take a look: the meat should be white throughout and steaming hot to the bone. Once you are happy that they are cooked, remove carefully using a slotted spoon and leave to drain on a tray lined with kitchen paper. Keep warm in an oven at 110°C/225°F/gas mark ¼. ———>

Meanwhile, combine the leftover marinade, the sugar, tamarind paste and 100ml (3½fl oz) of water in a saucepan and heat over a gentle heat, stirring together to ensure the sugar melts and the mixture combines. Mix the tablespoon of rice flour with 50ml (2fl oz) of cold water until smooth, then stir this into the sauce. Increase the heat and simmer for 6–8 minutes, stirring, until the flour is cooked out and the sauce has thickened to make a glaze. At this stage, slosh in a shot of whisky if you have it, then taste the glaze, it should be sweet, salty and moreish (bearing in mind it will be intense without the chicken). Add a little more sugar and tamarind if it's not sweet enough for you. Once you are happy with the taste, toss the deep-fried wings with the glaze in a large bowl, coating each chicken wing completely, then stack the wings neatly on a serving plate.

To serve, pour over any remaining glaze and sprinkle with the mint, coriander and **2 thinly sliced long red chillies**. It's probably best to serve these with finger bowls of warm water and a load of napkins if you don't want to chicken-up the house.

WHOLE BLISTERED BANANA CHILLIES STUFFED WITH PORK & TOMATO RELISH

This recipe uses a slightly simplified version of a paste, which is not an easy task as most Thai curry pastes have 10–20 ingredients. Known as "nahm prik ong" in Thailand, this relish is essentially a rich tomato and pork mixture that is served with raw vegetables and fresh herbs to dip. You can use 3 regular peppers or sweet long peppers if you can't find banana chillies (also known as Turkish chillies outside Asia).

Feeds 3–4. Gluten-free

400g (14oz) fatty minced pork	100g (3½oz) cherry tomatoes, halved	20g (¾oz) galangal or ginger, peeled and roughly chopped	1 lemongrass stalk, tough outer layer removed, sliced as thinly as possible	3 banana shallots, diced	3 tablespoons palm sugar (or 1½ tablespoons caster sugar)	8 large banana chillies, tops sliced off but reserved, deseeded

First, halve, then soak **10 dried long red chillies** in boiling water from the kettle for 30 minutes to soften, then drain.

Next, make the paste and tenderize the meat. In a large mixing bowl, mix the minced pork with the tomatoes, massaging the two together using your hands, then set aside while you make the paste (the acid in the tomatoes will tenderize the pork, allowing for a better mouthfeel once fried).

To make the paste, you will need a large granite pestle and mortar. Start by pounding the soaked, dried red chillies until they resemble a smooth paste (this takes longer than you might think). Scrape the chilli paste into a bowl and set aside. Next, do the same in turn with the galangal, lemongrass, **5 thinly sliced garlic cloves**, and then the shallots, pounding them individually into a paste. Once all the ingredients have been pounded, return them to the mortar and pound for a further 5–8 minutes until you have a smooth, red curry paste.

To make the relish, heat **100ml (3½fl oz) of vegetable oil** in a large frying pan until hot. Add the curry paste and fry over a high heat, moving it constantly to ensure that it does not stick and burn. Keep frying over a high heat, moving it constantly, for 10–15 minutes until the paste begins to darken a little and the ingredients no longer smell raw. ⟶

Once the paste starts to darken, add the pork mix and continue to fry hard and move regularly until all the pork is cooked through and combined with the paste. De-glaze the pan with **3 tablespoons of fish sauce**, then add the sugar, fry out for a few minutes, allowing it to caramelize and darken the meat a little more. When you are happy, taste the relish, it should be spicy, sweet and salty. If you want to adjust the seasoning to suit your taste, do it now. Remove from the heat, then skim off the excess fat/oil and reserve.

Now it's time to stuff and cook the banana chillies (or peppers). Using a tablespoon, spoon the mixture into the banana chillies (or peppers), dividing it evenly. Once stuffed, gloss them with the leftover fat/oil from cooking and sprinkle with a little salt, then place the chilli (or pepper) lids back on.

Preheat the grill to high. Place the chillies (or peppers) under the grill for 8–10 minutes, turning them halfway through. Alternatively, these can be cooked over a hot barbecue for 8–10 minutes, or in a preheated oven at 200°C/400°F/gas mark 6 for 20 minutes.

Remove the chillies from the grill and allow to cool a little before serving. Serve two stuffed chillies per person (or one stuffed pepper per person), and if you're in a party mood, just eat them with your hands and a napkin, otherwise, you can also serve them on a plate with steamed jasmine rice and a nice salad.

CITRUS CEVICHE SEABASS WITH SOUR FRUIT & DILL

This is a lovely dish when the weather is hot. I've chosen seabass in this recipe, but it works brilliantly with prawns or salmon, too, just apply the same process but change the fish. I make a chilli and lime dressing, known as "nahm yum" in Thailand, and use the acid from the lime to cook the fish rather than using any heat. The results are incredible, and the method makes this dish very quick and simple, with hardly any washing up. When eating fish in this way, it's a great time to really let the produce do the talking, so aim to get the best quality, freshest fish you can.

Feeds 2. Gluten-free

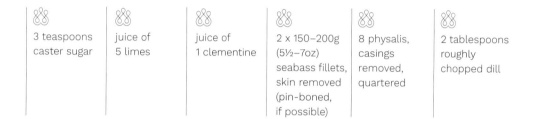

3 teaspoons caster sugar	juice of 5 limes	juice of 1 clementine	2 x 150–200g (5½–7oz) seabass fillets, skin removed (pin-boned, if possible)	8 physalis, casings removed, quartered	2 tablespoons roughly chopped dill

Start by preparing the nahm yum dressing. Using a pestle and mortar, pound together **2 peeled garlic cloves** and **3 long green chillies** into a coarse paste, using the caster sugar as an abrasive. Stir in the juice from 3 limes, the clementine juice and **3 tablespoons of fish sauce**, then taste. The dressing should taste sweet, salty, spicy and sour in equal measure, so adjust accordingly.

Next, using your sharpest knife, slice the seabass. Lay the seabass on a board and slice the fillets at a 75-degree angle to the board, with each slice measuring no more than 1cm (½in) in thickness. Place these slices into a glass mixing bowl, pour over the remaining lime juice, then toss the fish slices gently through the lime juice, ensuring that all the fish is coated. Leave for 3 minutes to let them get to know each other. You will notice during this time that the seabass will go from a clear white colour to a cloudy, opaque colour – this is a sign that the acid in the lime juice has done its job and the fish is ready for eating. Remove the fish from the lime juice, carefully shaking off any excess.

To serve, place the seabass slices flat on a plate, drizzle each piece with the nahm yum dressing and then sprinkle the plate with the chopped physalis and dill. You can add any other sour fruit of your choice, instead of or as well as, the physalis, if you like. This ceviche is delicious bulked out with some steamed jasmine rice on the side.

CHILLI, SOY & GARLIC KALE CRISPS

This is a bloody easy recipe, which shows off how tasty kale can be, with next to no work. Put it in a soup or stir-fry, pickle it, steam it, pan-fry it, deep-fry it, or as I do in this recipe, roast it. If you buy it and it's a little bitter, stick it in the freezer for a few hours to help sweeten and soften the leaves, making them delicious to eat and easier to cook.

Feeds 2–3. Vegetarian, vegan, gluten-free (use seaweed sauce or gluten-free soy sauce, if you like)

1¼ teaspoons white peppercorns	30–40g (1–1½ oz) ginger, peeled and roughly chopped	100ml (3½fl oz) light soy sauce	50g (1¾oz) light soft brown sugar	4 tablespoons sesame oil	250g (1lb 2oz), kale, thick stems removed and discarded, leaves ripped into 4–8cm (1½–3¼in) pieces

Lightly toast the peppercorns in a dry pan over a low heat for 3–5 minutes, then cool and grind to a fine powder using a pestle and mortar.

Using the same pestle and mortar or a food processor, combine **4 peeled garlic cloves**, the ginger and **3 roughly chopped long red chillies**, then pound together or process to a paste, using a little flaked sea salt as an abrasive. Stir in the soy sauce, 1 teaspoon of the ground white pepper, the sugar and sesame oil. Tip into a saucepan and cook over a medium heat for 5 minutes to melt the sugar. Set aside to cool.

Preheat the oven to 110°C/225°F/gas mark ¼ and line a large baking tray with baking parchment.

Using both hands, toss the kale through the cooled marinade, coating every piece. Excess marinade will fall off the kale and this can be reused to make more immediately, or kept in an airtight container in the fridge for 5–6 months.

Transfer the coated kale to the lined baking tray, ensuring it doesn't overlap too much. Bake for 1 hour, then check every 10 minutes or so until it is crisp – it usually takes 1½–2 hours in total. Keep checking it regularly because if it is left for too long it will turn brown and taste bitter.

Once crispy, remove from the oven, sprinkle the crisps with the remaining white pepper, then serve immediately. Once cool, they will keep in an airtight container for weeks and can be nibbled on as a snack, perfect with a sweet chilli dip, such as the Green Sweet Chilli Dipping Sauce (see page 145), or used as a garnish on curries or soups.

CRISPY PORK BELLY & PICKLED WATERMELON SALAD

I first put this combination together was when I was heading-up the Smoking Goat in London's Soho. The crispy, salty crackling from the pork belly, accompanied by the sweet, gentle and soft pickled watermelon, make for a pretty banging feed.

Feeds 2. Gluten free

250g (9oz) piece of pork belly, ribs removed, skin on	150ml (¼ pint) white vinegar	4 tablespoons sesame oil	3 tablespoons caster sugar	80g (2¾oz) watermelon flesh, chopped into bite-sized chunks	small handful of mint, leaves picked and torn	small handful of coriander, leaves picked

First, prepare and cook the pork belly. Submerge the pork belly in cold salted water in a deep saucepan, bearing in mind that it will expand and almost double in size during cooking, so ensure it is in deep water with enough cooking room. Place a lid on top, then simmer over a medium heat for 30–40 minutes until the belly is hot throughout and soft (it should have a core temperature of 75–80°C/167–176°F). Remove the pork from the water and set aside to cool on a wire rack.

Preheat the oven to 200°C/400°F/gas mark 6.

Once the pork is cool, score the skin with a sharp knife and rub in 50ml (2fl oz) of the vinegar and a good pinch of sea salt, ensuring you coat all of the skin. Place the pork belly on a baking tray on the middle shelf and roast for 30–40 minutes, or until the belly is juicy and moist within and the skin is golden brown and crispy. Remove from the oven, and when it's cool enough to handle, chop into bite-sized chunks and set aside.

Next, pickle the watermelon. In a small saucepan, combine the remaining vinegar, the sesame oil, caster sugar, a pinch of salt and 100ml (3½fl oz) of water and cook over a medium heat until the sugar has dissolved. Taste the liquor; it should be sweet and sour. Set aside to cool (or place the pan in a bowl of iced water, if you are in a hurry), then add the watermelon to the pickling liquor. The watermelon can be used immediately or left in the pickle for up to 30 minutes.

Using a slotted spoon, remove the watermelon from the pickling liquor and combine in a mixing bowl with the pork belly, mint and coriander and gently toss together, using a little of the pickling liquor to dress the herbs. Serve immediately with steamed jasmine rice.

LEMONGRASS, CHILLI & CARDAMOM PANCETTA

Making bacon at home is surprisingly easy and thoroughly delicious and this recipe comes courtesy of Jorge Thomas at Swaledale Foods. If you've also taken the time to smoke it at home, so much the better, but it will be nearly as good without. The pancetta can be used in sandwiches, braises and stir-fries. Try to source a traditional breed of pig reared outdoors – the quality will surpass commercial pork by some margin. Saltpetre is not essential, but will benefit the colour and flavour of your pancetta. This produces a relatively sweet cure, but the sugar can be halved for a less sweet result.

Makes 2kg (4lb 8oz). Gluten free

2 star anise	10 green cardamom pods	25g (1oz) dark soft brown sugar	1g (a pinch of) saltpetre (available online or replace with table salt)	2kg (4lb 8oz) boneless, skinless pork belly	2 fat lemongrass stalks, tough outer layer removed, roughly chopped

Blitz the star anise and cardamom pods together, ideally in a spice grinder, but a pestle and mortar would work, too. Combine the resulting spice powder with the sugar, 30g (1oz) sea salt and the saltpetre (or extra salt). Scatter this all over your piece of pork belly, taking care to work it into any nooks and crannies.

Using a pestle and mortar, pound the lemongrass heavily, before adding **3 long red chillies**, then pound together briefly. Massage this mixture on to the pork, then place it in an airtight container (or in a sealed plastic food/freezer bag, placed in a dish). The pork now needs 7 days in the fridge to cure – and you need to turn it every other day, bathing it in the brine that will have formed in the bottom of your chosen vessel.

For the next stage, you will need a piece of muslin cloth or a clean tea towel. Rinse and thoroughly dry the bacon, before double-wrapping it in the muslin or tea towel and tying it up. Hang the meat in a cool, airy and dry place for at least 2 days, but 10–14 days is better still. Pancetta can be hung to dry just about anywhere, but is best hung somewhere with a little humidity, such as above a sink in a kitchen or basement. If a suitable spot doesn't spring to mind, a fridge would be ok, although this tends to be a touch damp (a bloom or white mould may occur, much like salami, but this isn't something to be alarmed about). If you intend to smoke your bacon, 12 hours in cold wood smoke is ideal. Once smoked, it will keep for a long time wrapped in the fridge, however, for best results, use within 3 months or freeze it and slice when you want to use it. It can be stored for a further 3 months in the freezer but will start to lose flavour.

HEAVENLY BEEF JERKY

Known as "nua sawan" in Thai, heavenly beef jerky is essentially a sweet and spicy biltong. It is usually made on the sweet side so it can be nibbled on as a treat and because sugar acts as a preservative. Snacking is fundamental to Thai culture: many treats are eaten on the go and this is also tasty eaten with a bag of sticky rice.

Feeds 2–3

1 tablespoon coriander seeds	200g (7oz) beef – onglet, silverside or bavette	2 tablespoons palm sugar (or light soft brown sugar)	2 pinches of ground white pepper	3 tablespoons kecap manis

Lightly toast the coriander seeds in a dry pan over a low heat for a few minutes, then cool and gently pound using a pestle and mortar.

To prepare the beef, trim all the sinew and any unwanted hard fat from the meat. Slice into 4cm (1½in) squares, roughly 5mm (¼in) thick, then set aside.

Next, using a pestle and mortar, pound **2 peeled garlic cloves** to a paste, then add the palm sugar, white pepper, kecap manis and **1 teaspoon of fish sauce** and continue to pound until the mixture comes together to make a thick marinade. Scrape the marinade into a mixing bowl, add the beef pieces and mix thoroughly using your hands until the beef is well coated. Cover the worktop with a large piece of clingfilm, then dust the surface of the clingfilm with half the crushed coriander seeds. Place the beef slices on top in a single layer, then sprinkle the remaining crushed coriander over the top. Place another piece of clingfilm on top and gently roll over with a rolling pin, pushing the coriander seeds into the pieces of beef, then remove and discard the clingfilm.

Preheat the oven to 75–80°C/167–176°F/gas mark as low as you can go.

Lay the beef slices over a large grill tray in a single layer. Dry out in the oven with the door slightly ajar to allow any moisture to escape during the drying process. Dry the pieces for 3–4 hours, or until the meat begins to darken in colour and resembles the texture of jerky. Once ready, remove from the oven and leave to cool. At this stage, the beef can be stored in an airtight container for up to a week or frozen for up to 2 months.

To finish the jerky, heat **700ml (1¼ pints) of vegetable oil** in a deep, heavy-based pan over a medium heat to 180°C (350°F). A piece of beef should bubble gently and float on the surface, turning a light golden-brown colour within about 30 seconds when the oil is hot enough. Deep-fry the beef, a small handful at a time, for about a minute until golden brown, then remove using a slotted spoon and drain on kitchen paper, while you cook the remaining beef. Leave to cool for a minute or so. It's delicious still warm or cold.

KAFFIR & CHILLI CORN ON THE COB WITH CRUSHED CASHEW NUTS

This must be one of the easiest dishes to pull out of the bag, ever. I've used coconut oil to lather the seasoning over the corn on the cob, to keep it vegan. However, if you replace the coconut oil with butter, it also makes for a delicious lunch. I like it spicy, as you can see from the amount of bird's eye chillies used. For me, the spice is important in this recipe to balance the natural sweetness of the corn, but you can reduce the amount of chilli, if you prefer.

Feeds 2. Vegetarian, vegan, gluten-free

4 tablespoons coconut oil, gently melted	2 kaffir lime leaves, finely sliced	4 corn on the cob	2 tablespoons roasted cashew nuts, lightly pounded or roughly chopped

In a large mixing bowl, combine the coconut oil, lime leaves, **2 thinly sliced garlic cloves** and **4 finely chopped red or green bird's eye chillies**, then add the corn cobs. Using your hands, massage the seasoning into the corn cobs, taking your time and ensuring that every part is jammed full of the seasoning. Sprinkle a pinch of sea salt evenly over all the corn cobs, it should stick to the coconut oil with ease.

For best results, roast the cobs over a medium heat on a preheated barbecue for 15–20 minutes, turning them regularly to ensure even cooking. The corn will be golden brown and softened when it's ready to eat. Alternatively, you can roast them in the oven. Preheat the oven to 200°C/400°F/gas mark 6. Place the corn on a baking sheet and roast for 15–20 minutes.

Once the corn is ready, transfer to serving plates and sprinkle with the cashews, then serve. Bulk out with steamed jasmine rice and salad for a more filling lunch.

TIP
Cashew nuts can either be purchased pre-toasted or roasted at home. I always roast cashews in the oven for more even toasting. Preheat the oven to 110°C/225°F/gas mark ¼ and spread the cashews evenly over a baking tray. Roast on the middle shelf for 15–20 minutes until golden brown.

CRISPY TURMERIC SOFT-SHELL CRAB

There is no better way to prepare soft-shell crab than to fry it. A nice hot temperature creates a crispy, crunchy, salty outer layer, encasing the juicy taste of the sea hidden within, just waiting for you to take your first bite. This recipe is designed to snack on with a few drinks, but you can add the crispy crabs to salads, stir-fries, or even on top of soups and curries to add a textural component to the dish.

Feeds 2–3. Gluten free

| 6 soft-shell crabs (or 8 shell-on fresh raw tiger prawns) | about 20g (¾oz) turmeric, peeled and roughly chopped | about 20g (¾oz) ginger, peeled and chopped | 500ml (18fl oz) rapeseed oil, for deep-frying | 200g (7oz) cornflour | 1–2 limes, sliced into cheeks or wedges |

If the crabs are frozen, make sure they have completely thawed out, ideally overnight in the fridge (or by running them under a cold tap). Pat dry with kitchen paper.

Using a pestle and mortar, pound together **4 roughly chopped garlic cloves**, **1 roughly chopped long red chilli**, the turmeric and the ginger into a paste, using a pinch of sea salt as an abrasive (it doesn't matter if the paste is a little coarse as these little chunks will be delicious nuggets of flavour once fried). Add **4 teaspoons of fish sauce**. Alternatively, you can blitz it all in a food processor.

Coat the crabs thoroughly in the paste, ensuring you really rub the mix into the crabs, then place them on a tray. Leave to marinate either at room temperature for 30 minutes, or ideally, for 3 hours in the fridge.

Heat the rapeseed oil in a deep, heavy-based pan over a medium heat to around 180°C (350°F). Check the temperature of the oil by placing a discarded chilli stem or similar in the hot oil – if it bubbles gently and floats on the surface, then the oil is ready.

Meanwhile, sprinkle the cornflour over a tray and then carefully toss the crabs it, one at a time, until coated. Have a tray lined with kitchen paper at the ready.

Once the oil is hot enough, deep-fry the crabs, 2–3 at a time, for about 2 minutes on each side until golden brown and piping hot. Remove to the lined tray using a slotted spoon, and rest for 1 minute before serving. Repeat with the remaining crabs.

Sprinkle the crabs with salt and serve with the lime cheeks or wedges. If you like it saucy, serve with sweet fish sauce (see page 140) or sweet chilli sauce.

AROMATIC WHISKY-CURED SALMON WITH MANGO

This recipe was inspired by my travels in Thailand – a typical Koh Phangan tourist, drinking Mekhong (Thai spirit/rum) poured into buckets with ice and a mixer. Heavy amounts of alcohol, blended with herbs and spices, make this spirit delicious to cook with. In the restaurant, we like to drink it over ice with a slice of orange. If you can't get hold of Mekhong, just use your favourite whisky or rum.

Feeds 4–6 as a light nibble. Gluten-free

| 80g (2¾oz) caster sugar | zest of 3 limes, plus extra to serve | 40g (1½oz) turmeric, peeled and sliced | 2 tablespoons Mekhong spirit/rum | small handful of mint leaves, roughly chopped, plus extra to serve | 500g (1lb 2oz) salmon fillet, ideally in one piece, skin on | 1 ripe mango, peeled, stoned and thinly sliced |

First, make the cure. In a bowl, mix together **100g (3½oz) of coarse sea salt**, the sugar, lime zest, turmeric, whisky/rum and chopped mint. Mix all of this thoroughly until combined – if you have a food processor, give the mixture a quick whizz to let all the ingredients get to know each other properly.

Place a couple of layers of clingfilm on a work surface, ensuring that you have more than enough to completely wrap the salmon. Spoon a third of the cure into the centre of the clingfilm, then place the salmon on top, skin-side down. Cover the flesh side of the salmon with the remaining cure, making sure that all the fish is covered. Wrap the salmon tightly in the clingfilm, then refrigerate for 2 days – during this time the cure will penetrate and season all the flesh.

Once the curing time is up, remove the clingfilm and wash away the cure from the salmon under the cold running water, then pat the fish dry using kitchen paper.

Using your sharpest knife, slice the salmon as thinly as you can – ideally into 2–3mm (1/16–1/8in) thick slices. Slice into the flesh side first, slice down to the skin and then you can easily remove each slice from the underside of the skin. The cured slices can be stored in an airtight container in the fridge for up to a week, if you like.

Arrange the cured salmon on a plate with the mango slices placed amongst them and top with some extra mint leaves and lime zest. The fish will taste rich and salty, and cut through by the sweet, sharpness of the fresh mango and a little mint.

POMELO SALAD

Known as "yum som-o" in Thailand, pomelo salad is one of my favourites. It's simple to make and so explosive with flavour that you will be surprised you've made it in minutes using only a pestle and mortar and your hands. I've added fried garlic for texture, but if you are in a rush, this can be skipped. Pomelos are the largest citrus fruit on the planet and taste somewhere between a grapefruit and an orange while remaining unique. There really is nothing else quite like them.

Feeds 2. Vegetarian, vegan, gluten-free (use seaweed sauce or gluten-free soy sauce)

3 teaspoons caster sugar	juice of 3 limes	juice of 1 clementine	½ pomelo, peeled and chopped into large chunks	small handful of mint leaves	small handful of coriander leaves

Using a pestle and mortar, pound **8 peeled garlic cloves** into a coarse paste. Heat **500ml (18fl oz) of vegetable oil** in a deep, heavy-based pan over a medium heat to 180°C (350°F). To test the temperature of the oil, place a discarded chilli stem or similar in the hot oil and see how it reacts. It should bubble gently and float on the surface when the temperature is about right (if it's too hot, it will burn straight away; if it's too cool, it will sink). When you're happy that the oil is at the correct temperature, carefully spoon in the minced garlic and fry for 2–3 minutes – keep an eye on it as you don't want it to burn and taste bitter. Once the garlic turns golden brown, remove from the oil using a slotted spoon or sieve and drain on kitchen paper.

Next, prepare the nahm yum dressing. Using a pestle and mortar, pound together **2 peeled garlic cloves** and **3 chopped long green chillies** into a coarse paste, using the caster sugar as an abrasive. Stir in the lime juice, **3 tablespoons of fish sauce** and the clementine juice, then taste. (If you're vegetarian or vegan swap the fish sauce for soy sauce, or gluten-free soy sauce if you're coeliac.) The dressing should taste sweet, salty, spicy and sour in equal measure, so adjust the taste, as required.

Gently toss the pomelo, mint and coriander in a bowl, then drizzle over some dressing and mix, but don't drench the salad – people can always add a little more if they like, but the pomelo and herbs want to express their own flavours through the dressing.

Serve with sprinkles of the fried garlic over the top and either sticky rice or steamed jasmine rice – I love it with either.

"SOM TAM", GREEN APPLE SALAD

"Som tam" has fast become one of the most widely eaten and popular salads to come out of Asia. It originates from Laos but now has many variations from different countries. With this version, to make it more accessible, the green papaya can be substituted for shredded green apple. It's packed full of sweet, salty, sour and spicy goodness, and although originally the heart of this salad is shrimps, it's delicious without. To make this the way the Thais do, you should have a large wooden pestle and mortar at home, because, in time, the flavours of the ingredients become engrained in the wood, making it the perfect vessel to pound out a delicious salad.

Feeds 2–3. Vegetarian, vegan, gluten-free (use seaweed sauce or gluten-free soy sauce)

200g (7oz) shredded, cored green dessert apples or papaya flesh	15–20g (½–¾oz) palm sugar (or dark soft brown sugar)	2 tablespoons light soy sauce	4 tablespoons thick tamarind paste	juice of 1 lime	½ lime, chopped (zest left on)

Using a pestle and mortar, pound **2 peeled garlic cloves** to a paste, using a little flaky sea salt as an abrasive. Add **2 red bird's eye chillies**, bruising them and opening them to release their flavour, then add the green apple, stirring all the ingredients in the mortar with a spoon in one hand and pounding them together with a pestle in the other – this distributes the flavours thoroughly.

Add the palm sugar, soy sauce, tamarind paste, lime juice and chopped lime and give the salad a final bruise to ensure that all ingredients are packed full of the flavoursome dressing, checking that the palm sugar has been completely dissolved in the dressing.

Taste the dressing, it should be sweet, salty, sour and spicy with a hint of bitterness from the lime zest, and adjust to suit your taste, then serve. This salad is delicious eaten on its own or served with steamed jasmine rice for a big feed or as the perfect accompaniment to any curry or hearty meal, such as the Whole Spiced Yellow Crab Curry (see page 83) or King Oyster Mushroom Curry (see page 129).

CRISPY WHITEBAIT WITH GARLIC & TURMERIC

When I opened Farang two years ago, we took over my stepdad's, Marco's (otherwise known as Daddyo), Italian restaurant, the San Daniele, after he retired. It started as a pop-up and we didn't have a penny to our name, so all our money went into the staff and the food. We ended up building up a weird and wonderful reputation for being a Thai restaurant, which appeared to be a traditional Italian trattoria. In the San Daniele days, one of my favourite things to eat was the crispy whitebait, so here is my version to keep the name alive – R.I.P. the San Daniele.

Feeds 2. Gluten-free

10g (¼oz) turmeric, peeled (or 1 teaspoon ground turmeric)	5g (⅛oz) caster sugar	200g (7oz) whitebait (or small sardine or mackerel fillets)	100g (3½oz) cornflour	freshly ground black pepper, to taste

First, make the marinade. Using a pestle and mortar, pound together **3 peeled garlic cloves**, **3 red or green bird's eye chillies** and the turmeric to make a coarse paste, using a couple of pinches of salt as an abrasive (or blend them together using a food processor). Scrape the paste into a mixing bowl, then add the sugar and **4 teaspoons of fish sauce** and stir well. Add the whitebait and give them a good mix with your hands, ensuring they are all coated well, then cover and set aside at room temperature for 30 minutes, so the flavours can all get to know each other.

Heat **500ml (18fl oz) of vegetable oil** in a deep, heavy-based pan over a medium heat to around 180°C (350°F). Remove the whitebait from the marinade (discard the marinade) and transfer to a bowl with the cornflour, a pinch of salt and a small pinch of black pepper and toss thoroughly, making sure all the fish are well coated. Before frying the fish, check the oil is at the correct temperature by putting in one fish and see how it reacts. It should bubble gently and float on the surface, turning golden brown within 2–3 minutes. Deep-fry the fish in batches, a small handful at a time, until golden brown, then remove using a slotted spoon and drain on kitchen paper, while you cook the remainder. When all the fish has been fried, leave it to one side to rest for 2 minutes.

Serve the whitebait piled high in a serving bowl, topped with all the crispy bits and a good sprinkle of black pepper, plus a pinch of salt, if you like. These are delicious served with your favourite dipping sauce, such as the Roasted Chilli "Jaew" (see page 153).

"TOM YUM", AROMATIC CHILLI & GALANGAL SOUP

This is a brilliant winter soup. It's delicious eaten just as a soup, or with rice or noodles, so go nuts and decide for yourself. This recipe is the soup at its most basic level, but many things can be added, if you wish, from cherry tomatoes or roasted squash to wild mushrooms and pickles. Get a feel for it by following this recipe and once you are comfortable, get creative. It takes very little time to come together so is perfect for a quick hunger fix.

Feeds 2. Vegetarian, vegan, gluten-free (use seaweed sauce or gluten-free soy sauce)

600ml (20fl oz) vegetable stock	2–3 tablespoons light soy sauce	2 kaffir lime leaves	30–40g (1–1½oz) galangal, bruised using a pestle	1 lemongrass stalk, tough outer layer removed, chopped into 4cm (1½in) pieces and bruised	big pinch of Thai basil leaves	juice of ½ lime

Put the vegetable stock, 2 tablespoons of the soy sauce (add the remaining soy sauce later, if it needs it), a pinch of sea salt, the kaffir lime leaves, galangal, **2 green bird's eye chillies (bruised using a pestle and mortar)** and the lemongrass into a medium saucepan. Bring to a simmer, then simmer gently for 4–5 minutes until all the ingredients have softened with the flavours infused.

Finish by adding the Thai basil leaves and then dishing out into bowls, giving each bowl a good squeeze of lime juice. Check the seasoning, it should be salty, spicy, sour and aromatic with a hint of lime at the end, and adjust to suit your taste, if necessary. For added freshness, top with some Thai basil flowers, if you like.

"TOM KHA", COCONUT & GALANGAL SOUP

This is one of my all-time favourite soups and an absolute classic. In Thailand, it is eaten more in the style of a curry, with friendly ladles of the soup over jasmine rice shared amongst family and friends. This tasty version is created for simplicity, however, as with most Thai dishes, the possibilities are endless if you want to take it to the next level. Traditionally, poached chicken or prawns are added, "nam phrik pao" (chilli jam) adds a smokiness and spiciness to the soup, or the delicate umami flavour from mushrooms is also a winner.

Feeds 2. Vegetarian, vegan, gluten-free (use seaweed sauce or gluten-free soy sauce)

300ml (½ pint) vegetable stock	300ml (½ pint) coconut cream	2–3 tablespoons light soy sauce	40–50g (1½–1¾oz) piece of galangal, bruised using a pestle and mortar	1 lemongrass stalk, tough outer layer removed, chopped into 4cm (1½in) pieces and bruised	juice of ½ lime	big pinch of Thai basil leaves

Put the vegetable stock, 100ml (3½fl oz) of the coconut cream, 2 tablespoons of the soy sauce (add the remaining soy sauce later, if you feel it needs it), a pinch of sea salt, the galangal, **2 red or green bird's eye chillies (bruised using a pestle and mortar)** and the lemongrass in a medium saucepan. Bring to a simmer, then simmer gently for 4–5 minutes until all the ingredients have softened with the flavours infused.

Finish by stirring in the remaining coconut cream. Dish out into bowls, giving each bowl a good squeeze of fresh lime juice and topping with half the picked Thai basil before serving. Lastly, check the seasoning, it should be creamy, salty, a little spicy and aromatic with a sour edge from the lime, so adjust to suit your taste, if necessary. For added freshness, top with some Thai basil flowers, if you like.

MARINATED RAW BEEF & DILL

This dish is all about the beef, so make sure you buy the best you can, and try to get it aged a little, so the flavour has that next level of creaminess. The combination of natural sweetness from the meat with the sourness from the pickle, plus a kick of chilli and salt, means this dish is a banger of a starter. If you like, stir in the egg yolk and serve on toast or rice crackers to make a delicious canapé for a dinner party.

Feeds 2. Gluten-free

300g (10½oz) beef fillet (sirloin or rump)	4 Thai shallots, finely chopped	2 tablespoons chopped dill, plus extra for serving	1 tablespoon peeled and diced ginger	6 tablespoons pickled mustard greens, finely chopped (or pickled cabbage, cucumber or gherkin)	1 tablespoon coarsely ground black pepper	2 medium, free-range egg yolks

Trim the meat of any sinew or fat and then mince the meat as finely as possible using a sharp knife. Alternatively, you can pulse-blitz the meat in a food processor to mince it, but texturally, it will be better if diced by hand.

Next, make the marinade. In a large mixing bowl, combine the diced beef, the shallots, dill, ginger, **1 tablespoon of vegetable oil**, pickled mustard greens and black pepper and toss together well, making sure that the mix seasons the beef thoroughly.

Divide the beef between two serving plates and create a small well in the top of the beef mix. Place an egg yolk into each one.

Mix **3 tablespoons of fish sauce** and **3 finely chopped red or green bird's eye chillies** together to create "nahm pla" – a delicious salty and spicy condiment to serve alongside the marinated beef, so everyone can add as much spice and salt as they wish.

Serve sprinkled with a little more dill and the nahm pla on the side. For more of a fill, you can serve this with sticky rice to dip, or roti bread (see pages 53–55).

CONFIT DUCK & SWEET PLUM CRISPY WONTONS

Duck with sweet plum sauce is a delicious and classic combination and confit duck with sweet plum sauce packed into plump, golden brown, crispy wontons takes these flavours to another level. For best results, the duck should be cooked in duck fat (found in many supermarkets and butchers) but vegetable oil can be used instead, if you like.

Feeds 3–4 (Makes 12 wontons)

| 800ml (28fl oz) rendered duck fat (or vegetable oil, or use half duck fat and half vegetable oil) | 2 duck legs, skin on | about 30g (1oz) ginger, peeled and roughly chopped | 400g ripe plums, stoned and chopped into quarters | 50g (1¾oz) light soft brown sugar | 2 spring onions, roots and outer layers removed, finely sliced, white and green parts separated | 24 wonton wrappers (see Tip) |

Preheat the oven to 180°C/350°F/gas mark 4.

First, cook the duck legs. Gently melt the duck fat or heat the oil with a big pinch of salt in a nonstick, ovenproof pot over a low heat. Using a pestle and mortar, pound **2 peeled garlic cloves** into a coarse paste (or chop finely with a knife) and add this to the pot. Once the duck fat is melted/heated, remove from the heat and place the duck legs into the warm, melted fat, ensuring each leg is fully submerged (top up with a little more melted fat/oil, if necessary).

Place a cartouche (circle of nonstick baking parchment) on top of the duck legs, resting it on the surface of the fat (this will help to keep any moisture released during the cooking process in the pot for maximum flavour). Place the lid on the pot, transfer to the oven and cook for 4–5 hours. After 4 hours, take the legs out and check if they are cooked – when cooked, the leg meat should fall off the bone relatively easily. If they are not fully cooked, then return to the oven and check every 15 minutes or so until they are.

Remove from the oven and transfer the duck legs to a plate. Once cool enough to handle but still warm, shred the duck meat and skin from the bone as finely as you can and set aside. The bones can be frozen and used for stock at a later point or discarded. ⟶

Next, make the wonton filling. Using a pestle and mortar, make a paste from **2 peeled garlic cloves** and the ginger, or finely chop both with a knife. Measure about 100ml (3½fl oz) of the residual duck fat into a saucepan, add the paste and fry over a medium heat for 5–6 minutes until the paste begins to turn golden brown and smell fragrant.

Add the plums and fry gently for 15 minutes until they have started to break down and create a chunky plum sauce – add a dash of water to the pan at this stage to stop the paste frying any more. Stir in the brown sugar and cook gently for a further 5 minutes until the sugar has caramelized and the sauce has darkened a little.

Remove from the heat and fold through the spring onion greens, then tip into a heatproof bowl and set aside to cool. Once cool, combine this mixture with the shredded duck, adding a little more of the residual melted fat, if it's a little dry. Taste and add a little salt, if you like.

To assemble the wontons, divide the cooled filling into 12 equal portions, about 50g (1¾oz) per portion. Place 12 wonton wrappers on a flat surface and spoon a portion of the filling into the centre of each one. One at a time, moisten the edge of each wrapper using a pastry brush dipped in water or gently rubbing with your dampened finger, then place a second wrapper on top, enclosing the filling. Using your fingers, press the wrappers firmly together, enclosing the filling tightly within the wonton. Repeat to make all the filled wontons.

Finally, cook the wontons. Heat all the leftover fat from the duck confit in a deep, heavy-based pan over a medium heat to 180°C (375°F). Have a tray ready alongside lined with some kitchen paper. Test to see if the oil is hot enough by dropping in a little piece of a plain (unfilled) wonton wrapper, it should bubble gently and float on the surface, turning golden brown in about a minute.

Carefully add the filled wontons to the hot oil, three at a time, deep-frying for about a minute on each side until golden brown all over. Remove the cooked wontons from the oil using a slotted spoon and drain on the kitchen paper. Deep-fry the remaining wontons in batches as before.

Sprinkle the wontons with a little flaked sea salt and garnish with the remaining white spring onions. These are delicious eaten on their own or with a dipping sauce, such as the Spiced Sweet Plum Sauce (see page 146) and/or Pickled Cucumber & Apple (see page 150).

TIP

Wonton wrappers can be bought fresh or frozen from most Asian supermarkets or purchased online. Alternatively, filo pastry sheets, cut into 5cm (2in) squares make a suitable replacement, although for best results use wonton wrappers, if you can.

ROASTED GARLIC ROTI BREAD WITH ROSEMARY SALT

Roti bread has become a staple for me, and everyone I work with. It's actually a staple for customers at Farang, too, as people like it to mop up their curry and leftover sauce. Roti goes with salads, works as a starter, or instead of rice, and is commonly used to wrap fruits, chocolate and sweets as a dessert, too. For me, roti is as essential at a Thai dinner table as rice. However, Thai culture is built up around the importance of rice, which has always been a product of political, historical and cultural significance, so this roti theory is my own Farang view and mine alone. We started making 3kg (6lb 8oz) of roti a week in the restaurant two years ago, and we now sell about 70kg (154lb) a week, so if it keeps increasing at this rate, I may have to think about losing the bathrooms to make more room for roti production!

Makes 6 rotis. Vegetarian

150g (5½oz) unsalted butter, at room temperature	about 2 sprigs of rosemary, leaves picked and finely chopped	700g (1lb 9oz) plain flour	1 egg

Preheat the oven to 180°C/350°F/gas mark 4.

To make the roasted garlic butter, wrap **½ head of garlic (in the skin)** in foil, then roast it in the oven for 30 minutes until it has softened inside throughout. Once it's ready, a knife should gently slide in and out with ease. Remove from the oven and leave until cool enough to handle it, then squeeze the roasted flesh out of the cloves within the head, leaving the skins behind – you should have a lovely thick, pungent, golden-brown purée.

Melt the butter in a small pan with the roasted garlic purée and simmer gently for about 15 minutes until you can see that the clarified butter has split from the solids. Pour the clarified butter (shiny and slightly clear, rather than cloudy) into another container, ready for use when frying the roti, and keep the leftover sediment to use in the dough.

To make the rosemary salt, mix the chopped rosemary with **1 tablespoon of flaked sea salt**. It is best to combine these using a pestle and mortar or a spice grinder, if you can, but it's not essential. Any leftover salt is banging used on most dishes, so keep it on the table for a few days – it won't last long. ⟶

Next, make the roti dough. Sift the flour into a mixing bowl, make a well in the middle, then add the egg and the reserved garlic butter sediment. Using your hands, mix and rub together until the mix begins to resemble breadcrumbs. Next, while stirring with a fork, add 225ml (8fl oz) of warm water, little by little, until you have a tacky dough, then knead for about 5 minutes on a flat surface. The dough should be a little tacky but not sticking to the bowl or your hands. If it's too wet, add a little flour as you knead; if it's too dry, add a little more water (up to 125ml/4fl oz, if needed). This dough is quite loose compared to regular bread dough; if you poke it, the indent from your finger does not bounce back. Place the dough in a lightly oiled bowl, then oil the top of the dough. Cover with clingfilm, ensuring the clingfilm is in direct contact with the dough to stop it crusting over, then leave to rest for a minimum of 30 minutes and a maximum of 4 hours, at room temperature. This dough can be stored in the fridge for up to a week at this stage, but bring it back to room temperature slowly before using.

Now for the fun bit, cooking the roti. If you're feeling lucky, then try the traditional method by slapping out the roti dough. Lightly oil a clean surface. Divide the dough into 6 even portions and form each into a small ball (about the size of a golf ball). Next, place a dough ball on the oiled surface. Flatten it into a rough circle and gently lift the side closest to you and drag it towards you, then lift it quickly but delicately and slap it back on to the surface (the elasticity and stickiness of the dough means that it doesn't rip too easily and it stretches bigger as you drag it). Repeat this process until the dough is roughly 2–3mm (1/16–1/8in) thick (the thinner the better, and a few holes are fine). Alternatively, you can use a rolling pin, or just stretch it out with your hands. It's hard to get it perfect the first time, so don't worry if it all goes a little pear-shaped, it will still produce some tasty bread. Repeat with the remaining balls of dough.

Heat some of the clarified garlic butter in a large frying pan over a medium heat (the butter needs to be hot to crisp the dough). Delicately lift a piece of dough into the pan; if it sizzles, you're doing it right. Fry for about 1 minute on each side until the roti is golden brown and crispy on both sides. Remove to a tray lined with kitchen paper to drain off any excess butter, while you cook the remaining rotis in the same way. Serve warm, sprinkled with the rosemary salt to taste.

TIP

This dough can be used for sweet and savoury rotis, so use it however you like. You can also cook the dough on its own and dip it into curries. It's also great just to eat as a snack.

STIR-FRIES

STIR-FRIED CHICKEN WITH CASHEW NUTS & EGG NOODLES

This stir-fry is probably one of the most popular and common dishes to find in any "hole-in-the-wall" eatery across Thailand. Known as "gai phat met mamuang himmaphan", this dish is also typically stir-fried without noodles and served with steamed jasmine rice, which is equally as delicious.

Feeds 2. Vegetarian (if using sweet potato – see Tip)

| 200g (7oz) boneless, skinless chicken breasts, sliced into tablespoon-sized pieces | 2 eggs, cracked into a bowl | 150g (5½oz) fresh egg noodles (or dried noodles blanched until soft and refreshed in cold water) | 200ml (7fl oz) chicken (or vegetable) stock | pinch of caster sugar | 3 tablespoons oyster sauce | 3 tablespoons toasted cashew nuts |

In a bowl, mix **3 finely chopped garlic cloves** (alternatively, these can be ground to a paste using a pestle and mortar), **2 thinly sliced red bird's eye chillies**, the chicken (or sweet potato – see Tip), **1 tablespoon of vegetable oil** and the kecap manis. Massage together with your hands, ensuring all the chicken (or sweet potato) is covered.

Place a nonstick wok over a high heat and leave it to get really hot for a few minutes. Pour **2 tablespoons of vegetable oil** into the wok – the intense heat should ensure it is smoking hot immediately. With a wok spoon (or wooden spoon) in one hand, add the eggs, then leave to cook for 20 seconds before scraping around the wok – this will create chunks of egg like an omelette. Add the chicken (or sweet potato), garlic and chilli mixture and stir-fry for 2 minutes until all the chicken is sealed and the garlic is starting to turn golden brown. Add the noodles and stir-fry for a further minute, moving the noodles constantly to colour them without letting them stick to the wok. Next, add the stock, caster sugar, oyster sauce and cashews and stir-fry for a further minute to soften the cashews and ensure the chicken (or sweet potato) is cooked through.

Taste the juices with a teaspoon, they should be savoury and a little spicy with a touch of sweetness, so adjust if necessary. Serve in bowls with chopsticks.

TIP

For a vegetarian version, use vegetarian oyster sauce and replace the chicken with peeled sweet potatoes, chopped into 2cm (¾in) chunks, boiled until soft and then refreshed in cold water before stir-frying. Swap the chicken stock for vegetable stock.

SMOKY STIR-FRIED BEEF WITH CHILLI JAM & ONION

This recipe is one of the first stir-fries I was taught and for this reason sticks close to me as a favourite. It is incredibly important to have the wok explosively hot and to cook quickly. If you get the temperatures perfect, the beef will be rare in the middle, yet smoky and charred on the outside. Try it with venison, too.

Feeds 2. Gluten-free

| 4 banana shallots, unpeeled | 1 lemongrass stalk | 250g (9oz) beef steak, bavette or onglet, sliced across the grain into 3cm (1¼in) chunks | 1 white onion, sliced into 1cm (½in) chunks | 1 tablespoon white vinegar | 1 tablespoon palm sugar (or 1 teaspoon caster sugar) | 2 tablespoons tamarind paste |

Preheat the oven to 180°C/350°F/gas mark 4.

To make the chilli jam, place the banana shallots, lemongrass, ½ head of garlic (in the skin) and 3 long red chillies on a nonstick baking tray, then drizzle with 2 tablespoons of vegetable oil. Roast on the top shelf for 25–30 minutes until softened (the lemongrass may need a further 5–10 minutes).

Leave until cool enough to handle, then peel the skin off the garlic and shallots. Discard the skin and set the flesh to one side. Remove the stalks from the chillies and roughly chop, then remove the tough outer layer from the lemongrass and thinly slice. Using a granite pestle and mortar, pound everything together to make a coarse paste, or blitz in a food processor. This is your roasted chilli jam.

Heat 2 tablespoons of vegetable oil in a nonstick wok over a high heat until almost smoking hot. With a wok spoon (or wooden spoon) in one hand, stir-fry the beef and onion in the oil, gently moving them constantly to seal the meat on all sides and begin to caramelize the onion. Add the roasted chilli jam and continue to toss for a minute or so – you may need to scrape the wok as the jam will stick a little. After a minute or so, reduce the heat and deglaze the wok with 1 tablespoon of fish sauce, the vinegar, sugar and tamarind paste and stir well. Taste the stir-fry, it should be sweet, sour, salty, smoky and spicy, so adjust the seasoning as you prefer.

To serve, pile the beef into bowls along with all the juices and enjoy with steamed jasmine rice alongside. Serve with sliced cucumber and fresh coriander or Thai basil leaves to add a little colour and freshness, if you like.

STIR-FRIED MUSSELS WITH GINGER, WHITE PEPPER & THAI BASIL

We should eat more mussels. They are one of the most sustainable sources of protein from the ocean, due to the fact that their aquaculture is zero-input; in English, this means that they do not require any added feed or fertilizers to survive and they also reproduce very quickly, making them the perfect, guilt-free seafood meal. I think I could cook a different mussel stir-fry every day for a year before I needed to repeat a recipe, there are so many delicious combinations. This recipe is one of our favourite staff lunches at Farang, as it's really tasty and quick to assemble.

Feeds 2. Gluten-free

2 tablespoons turmeric, peeled and pounded to a paste	200g (7oz) fresh mussels in shell, scrubbed, beards and barnacles removed	25–30g (1oz) ginger, peeled and chopped into matchsticks	pinch of caster sugar	pinch of ground white pepper	150ml (¼ pint) fish stock	small handful of Thai basil leaves

First, prepare all your ingredients in separate bowls for easy access when cooking the stir-fry. Pound **3 peeled garlic cloves** to a paste using a pestle and mortar.

Heat **1 tablespoon of vegetable oil** in a nonstick wok until it is smoking hot, then add the garlic and turmeric and stir-fry for 30–40 seconds. Once the garlic begins to turn golden brown, add the mussels, placing them gently in the wok to ensure that none breaks on impact. Gently toss the mussels in the wok, allowing the heat to penetrate them all, then, once they start to open, add three-quarters of the ginger, the sugar, the white pepper, **1–2 tablespoons of fish sauce** and **2 thinly sliced (deseeded) long red chillies**, and gently move a wok spoon (or wooden spoon) around so that the flavours can all get to know each other.

Finally, add the fish stock and bring gently to the boil, then lightly stir in the Thai basil. Before serving, taste the broth, it should be sweet, salty, fishy, fresh and aromatic from the Thai basil, so adjust the seasoning to taste. Discard any mussels that haven't opened.

Serve the mussels in bowls sitting in the broth and top with the remaining ginger and some Thai basil flowers, if you like. Serve with steamed jasmine rice for more of a fill. And don't forget an empty bowl for the discarded shells and finger bowls of warm water.

PRAWN PAD THAI

This is the blueprint recipe for a tasty prawn pad Thai, but other great additions are tofu, Chinese chives, pickled mooli or turnip, fresh coriander and bird's eye chillies. If you exchange the prawns for sliced oyster mushrooms and the fish sauce for soy sauce, you have yourself a pretty banging vegetarian version.

Feeds 2. Gluten-free. Vegetarian (if using mushrooms and soy sauce – see above)

150g (5½oz) dried flat rice noodles, 5mm (¼in) thick	100g (3½oz) palm sugar	100ml (3½fl oz) thick tamarind paste	2 eggs, cracked into a bowl and beaten	6 fresh raw prawns, shells removed and deveined	10g (¼oz) toasted peanuts, semi-pounded using a pestle and mortar	1 lime, sliced into cheeks or wedges

Soak the rice noodles in cold water for at least 2 hours until softened (or according to the packet instructions), then drain.

Roast **4 long red chillies** in a dry nonstick wok over a medium heat for 3 minutes, stirring constantly, until they darken and smoke a little, then pound to a powder using a pestle and mortar. Set aside.

Put the palm sugar and tamarind paste in a medium saucepan and gently melt together over a medium heat, stirring occasionally, until no lumps of sugar remain.

Heat **50ml (2fl oz) of vegetable oil** in a large nonstick wok over a high heat, then add the eggs and cook for 10 seconds or so, then scrape to form chunks of omelette. Add the noodles and stir constantly. Spread them across the surface of the wok to ensure even cooking until they turn translucent. Move the noodles to one side of the wok, add a little more oil to the centre, then add the prawns and stir-fry for 1–2 minutes until they have turned pink. Toss all the ingredients back together in the wok.

Pour the tamarind sugar around the sides of the wok, ensuring that the sauce has direct contact with the heat of the wok and caramelizes as it trickles down into the noodles, then toss the noodles with the sauce. Reduce the heat and add **2 tablespoons of fish sauce** (or soy sauce, if you wish), 1 teaspoon of the chilli powder and half the peanuts and toss all the ingredients together.

Check the seasoning, it should be sweet, fishy and savoury, with a smoky chilli kick; if it's too sweet, add another tablespoon of fish sauce (or soy sauce). Serve immediately on a large plate with the remaining peanuts, chilli powder and lime cheeks or wedges for people to season according to their taste.

DRUNKEN NOODLES WITH TIGER PRAWNS & THAI BASIL

Known as "pad kee mao" in Thailand, drunken noodles are a great way to use up any bits and bobs you have in the fridge. You can add whatever vegetables or protein you like, it's tasty with braised duck, chicken or crab. I've never known why it's called drunken noodles, so I sometimes add a shot of whisky to ensure it makes more sense!

Feeds 2. Vegetarian (if using vegetarian oyster sauce and mushrooms – see Tip)

100g (3½oz) flat rice noodles (fresh are best)	6 fresh raw tiger prawns, outer shells removed and deveined	2 eggs, cracked into a bowl	3 tablespoons palm sugar, pounded in a mortar so there are no lumps	3 tablespoons oyster sauce	1 head of pak choi, core removed and thinly sliced	small handful of Thai basil leaves

If the noodles are dried, check the packet instructions, as you may need to soak them in water for an hour to soften before stir-frying; if so, once soaked, drain thoroughly.

Pound **2 roughly chopped bird's eye chillies** and **2 peeled garlic cloves** to a coarse paste using a pestle and mortar. Heat **2 tablespoons of vegetable oil** in a nonstick wok and leave over a high heat for a minute or so until it is smoking hot. Add the noodles and spread them across the heat of the wok, then toss them regularly for 30 seconds or so until they begin to turn translucent and soften. Move them to one side of the wok, add **another tablespoon of oil**, then add the garlic and chilli paste with the prawns (or mushrooms – see Tip). Stir-fry for 1½–2 minutes until the paste begins to turn golden brown and the prawns have turned pink. Pour the eggs over the top, leave them to scramble for a few seconds and then move them a little to avoid burning.

When the eggs are cooked, mix everything with the noodles, then add **3 tablespoons of fish sauce** (or soy sauce, if you prefer), the palm sugar and oyster sauce and toss through the noodles. Continue to stir-fry for a further minute or so and these liquids will cook the (fresh) noodles and season the stir-fry. Turn the heat off and taste, it should be sweet, salty and moreish, so adjust as necessary.

To serve, gently fold the pak choi and Thai basil leaves into the noodles and serve in bowls with chopsticks. Squeeze over a little lime juice, if you wish.

TIP
Swap the prawns for king oyster mushrooms for a vegetarian alternative. Use 6 mushrooms, sliced into 1cm (½in) thick slices, and cook as for the prawns above.

CRISPY TOFU WITH COCONUT CREAM & THAI BASIL

Tofu is so versatile, and when squeezed of its liquid, it becomes a great binding ingredient, which is almost meat-like in texture, making it the perfect addition to many vegan dishes. Frying it before stir-frying is best, as with a piece of meat it seals the tofu, giving it crunch on the outside, with a juicy texture within.

Feeds 2. Vegetarian, vegan, gluten-free (if using gluten-free soy sauce)

200g (7oz) fresh firm tofu, drained and chopped into bite-sized chunks	1 banana shallot, finely sliced	200ml (7fl oz) coconut cream	small pinch of caster sugar	1 tablespoon light soy sauce	40g (1½oz) ginger, peeled and chopped into matchsticks	small handful of Thai basil leaves

Pour **400ml (14fl oz) of vegetable oil** into a non-stick wok and heat over a medium heat to around 180°C (350°F). To check the temperature, place a piece of tofu into the hot oil and see how it reacts. It should bubble gently and float on the surface and turn golden brown and crispy after about 2 minutes of frying; if it sinks it is not hot enough and if it burns within a minute, the oil is too hot, so adjust accordingly.

Add the tofu to the hot oil and deep-fry for about 2 minutes until golden brown and crispy. Remove using a slotted spoon and drain on kitchen paper to remove the excess oil. Carefully pour the hot oil into a heatproof container and set aside – this can be used again in the future.

Place the wok back over a high heat (the residual oil left in the wok should be enough to stir-fry with, but add a touch more if there is not a little pool in the centre). Once the oil is hot, add the banana shallot and stir-fry until translucent. Stir in the coconut cream, sugar, soy sauce, tofu and half the ginger and continue to simmer until the coconut cream has reduced and thickened to make a delicious sauce.

Gently fold in the Thai basil and taste, it should be salty, sweet and fragrant from the basil, but adjust to suit your taste. Serve in bowls, accompanied by some steamed jasmine rice, with the resmaining ginger scattered over to garnish, along with some Thai basil flowers, if available.

GRILLED DUCK LARB

"Larb", sometimes spelt "laap" or "laab", essentially means a minced meat salad. It is very typical of the Isan provinces in the north eastern region of Thailand. Salty, spicy, smoky and sour, it is an absolute classic eaten with sticky rice.

Feeds 2-3. Gluten-free

2 boneless duck breasts (skin on), plus 1 duck liver and 1 heart (optional)	1 tablespoon caster sugar	juice of 2 limes	1 teaspoon cumin seeds, lightly toasted and ground	small handful of mint leaves, torn in half	small handful of coriander leaves	2 tablespoons dry sticky rice, toasted and ground

Roast **4 dried long red chillies** in a dry nonstick wok over a medium heat for 3 minutes, until they harden darken, crisp and darken a little. Leave to cool, then grind to a powder.

Prepare the duck. Place the offal (if using) in a bowl and coat in **2 tablespoons of vegetable oil** and a small pinch of salt, massaging them with your hands.

Place the duck breasts, skin-side down, in a hot griddle pan over a medium-high heat, or over a preheated medium-hot barbecue, and griddle/grill for 3 minutes untouched. Once the skin is golden brown, flip the breasts and seal the undersides for a further 2–3 minutes. Remove to a plate and set aside to rest (this will be very rare, but you can cook it for a bit longer, if you prefer). Now griddle or barbecue the liver and heart – these shouldn't take more than a minute on either side – then rest with the duck breasts.

While the duck is still warm, slice all of the flesh and skin into thin slices, then, using a meat cleaver, mince the meat and the offal together to make a delicious juicy mixture. If you're not happy with how rare the duck is but have already minced it, just toss it through a hot wok for a minute or so until it is cooked to your liking.

Mix the duck with the sugar, stirring to melt the sugar in the residual heat of the duck, then add **1 tablespoon of fish sauce**, the lime juice, chilli powder (halve the amount if you don't like it too hot), the ground cumin, mint and coriander. Dish up in bowls, dusted with the toasted rice to add texture and crunch. Serve with Baby Gem lettuce leaves to scoop it up, if you want to impress.

TIP
To toast dry sticky rice, toast the uncooked grains in a dry nonstick wok over a medium heat for 8–10 minutes until golden brown, then tip into a bowl and cool before pounding to a powder using a pestle and mortar.

SPICY WILD MUSHROOM NOODLES

Known as "pad hed", stir-fried mushrooms are a common meal eaten across Thailand. Mushrooms, especially chunky ones, such as king oyster or shimeji, are amazing at collecting the smokiness from the wok and holding on to the flavour, making them the perfect ingredient for grilling or stir-frying.

Feeds 2. Vegan (if vegetarian, use fresh egg noodles instead of rice noodles)

150g (5½oz) dried flat rice noodles	200g (7oz) mixed wild mushrooms, larger mushrooms chopped into 2cm (¾in) chunks	50g (1¾oz) hispi cabbage, sliced into 1cm (½in) chunks	roughly 20g (¾oz) ginger, peeled and chopped into matchsticks	1 tablespoon vegan oyster sauce (usually made from mushrooms)	pinch of caster sugar	pinch of toasted and ground white peppercorns (see page 27)

Soak the rice noodles in cold water for a few hours or overnight to soften (or according to the packet instructions), then drain.

Roast **2 long red chillies** in a dry nonstick wok over a medium heat for 3 minutes, stirring constantly, until they darken and smoke a little. Set aside to crisp up.

Place a nonstick wok over a high heat and leave for a few minutes to get smoking hot. This is the best way to resemble the heat of a wok burner.

Add **3 tablespoons of vegetable oil** to the wok, the heat should immediately make the oil smoke a little. Into this add the thick mushrooms and stir-fry, moving them gently and constantly with a wok spoon (or wooden spoon), allowing the heat to touch all sides of the mushrooms and creating a little smoke within the wok, which will help to add flavour to the stir-fry. After about a minute, when the mushrooms are beginning to char a little, add **3 finely chopped garlic cloves**, the cabbage, noodles, half the ginger and the smaller mushrooms and continue to stir-fry in the same fashion for a further minute until all the mushrooms and vegetables are browning and hot throughout.

Finally, add 200ml (7fl oz) of water, the oyster sauce, caster sugar, white pepper and crispy chillies, breaking them in with your fingers (do wash your hands afterwards). Taste for seasoning; the juices should be a little sweet, salty, smoky, spicy, savoury and umami, so adjust to suit your taste. Serve the stir-fry in bowls with the remaining ginger sprinkled over to garnish.

HOME-STYLE CABBAGE STIR-FRIED WITH CHILLI, WHITE PEPPER & SOY

This is a dish that my sous chef Dan and I have been obsessed with since we first tasted it at a restaurant called Silk Road in Camberwell, south London. The smokiness from the wok and the pure fire in your mouth from the heaps of chillies, make it one of those dishes that you can't stop piling on to your rice. You would never have thought that plain old cabbage can so quickly be transformed into something this glorious and tasty.

Feeds 2. Vegetarian, vegan, gluten-free (use seaweed sauce or gluten-free soy sauce, if you like)

2 tablespoons peeled and roughly chopped turmeric	small pinch of ground white peppercorns	200g (7oz) white cabbage, chopped into bite-sized chunks	1 teaspoon caster sugar	2 tablespoons light soy sauce	100ml (3½fl oz) vegetable stock

Soak **6 dried long red chillies** in boiling water from the kettle for 30 minutes until softened, then drain, chop into 1cm chunks and set aside.

Place a large, nonstick wok over the highest heat and leave it for 2–3 minutes so the surface becomes as hot as possible.

Meanwhile, gather your ingredients. Using a pestle and mortar, pound together **4 peeled garlic cloves**, the turmeric and white pepper to create a coarse paste. Next, assemble all your ingredients within arm's reach.

Drop **2 tablespoons of vegetable oil** into the hot wok and spread it out, it should be so hot that it smokes a little straight away, then add the cabbage and stir-fry, ensuring that the oil is coating every piece of cabbage. After a few minutes, the cabbage will start to soften and turn a little transparent, so at this point, add the turmeric and garlic paste, the chopped dried chillies and **2 long red fresh chillies (sliced into rings)** and continue to toss in the wok constantly until all the garlic has turned golden brown.

Reduce the heat to low and add the sugar, give this a little toss through the ingredients – the residual heat from the cabbage should caramelize the sugar quickly. Add the soy sauce and stock and give it all one final toss to combine the ingredients. It should be smoky, sweet, salty and proper spicy. It's perfect served with steamed jasmine rice.

STIR-FRIED CHILLI SHRIMPS WITH THAI BASIL & FRESH LIME

In Thailand, this dish is known as "pad krapow kung" and is as quick to make as it is delicious. As with any stir-fry, it is important to ensure that you have a smoking hot wok to start with and all of your ingredients prepared and in bowls at arm's length from the wok, so you can manage the dish with speed and precision.

Feeds 2

200g (7oz) fresh raw shrimps or prawns, shelled, deveined and cleaned (leave the heads on, if you like)	1 tablespoon oyster sauce	⅔ tablespoon caster sugar	small handful of Thai basil, leaves picked	½ teaspoon ground white peppercorns	1 lime, sliced into cheeks or wedges

First, arrange all your ingredients, minus the lime, within arm's reach of the hob and place a large nonstick wok over a high heat. Leave the wok over the heat for a few minutes so it becomes smoking hot.

Next, using a pestle and mortar, pound together **2 peeled garlic cloves** and **2 sliced red bird's eye chillies** to make a coarse paste, or finely chop them together on a board.

Add **2 tablespoons of vegetable oil** to the wok by pouring it around the sides and allowing it to spread to the middle. Next, add the shrimps or prawns and gently toss in the wok for 1 minute until they have turned pink. Add the garlic and chilli paste and toss for about 30 seconds so that the paste begins to turn golden brown and the shrimps/prawns have a slight golden-brown char on them.

Reduce the heat to low and deglaze the wok with **1 tablespoon of fish sauce** and the oyster sauce. Add the sugar and toss the shrimps/prawns to ensure they are all coated in the sugar – the heat from the wok should caramelize the sugar and the stir-fry will begin to darken slightly.

Finish by adding all the Thai basil and the white pepper. Toss the herbs gently through the wok, then serve with steamed jasmine rice and the lime cheeks or wedges ready to squeeze over the shrimps/prawns. Serve with finger bowls of warm water, if you're serving the shellfish with the heads on.

STIR-FRIED GLASS NOODLES WITH BROCCOLI AND CRISPY GARLIC

In Thailand, stir-fried glass noodles are known as "phat wun sen". Traditionally, they are cooked with chicken, oyster sauce and vegetables, however, this vegan version always goes down a storm. For added richness, get your hands on some vegetarian oyster sauce, a dollop of that in this stir-fry gives it a lip-smacking umami hit.

Feeds 2. Vegetarian, vegan, gluten-free (use seaweed sauce or gluten-free soy sauce)

200g (7oz) dried glass noodles (or mung bean noodles)	100g (3½oz) tenderstem broccoli	1 teaspoon caster sugar	2 tablespoons light soy sauce	20g (¾oz) roasted peanuts, roughly chopped	small handful of Thai basil leaves	juice of 1 lime

Put the glass noodles in a bowl, cover with room temperature water and leave to soften for 10 minutes, then refresh in cold water and drain.

Finely chop **6 garlic cloves** or pound them to a paste using a pestle and mortar. In a small, deep saucepan, heat **300ml (½ pint) of vegetable oil** over a medium heat to around 180°C (350°F). To check the temperature, place a small amount of garlic into the hot oil, it should bubble gently and float on the surface. Add all the garlic into the hot oil and fry for 4–5 minutes until the garlic is golden brown.

Place a metal sieve over a heatproof bowl and carefully pour the garlic through the sieve to separate it from the oil, then tease it apart with a fork. Drain the garlic on kitchen paper and set aside. Cool and store any leftover oil, and use instead of vegetable oil.

Cook the broccoli in a pan of lightly salted boiling water for 3–4 minutes until vibrant green and softened slightly but with a little crunch.

Meanwhile, place a few tablespoons of garlic oil in a nonstick wok over a high heat. Using a slotted spoon, remove the broccoli from the boiling water and place it into the wok, then stir-fry for a minute or two, so it browns a little. Add the glass noodles and stir-fry for a further minute. Add the sugar and soy sauce and stir into the noodles, allowing them to caramelize. Remove from the heat and add the peanuts, Thai basil, **2 finely sliced long red chillies** and the lime juice, then fold together.

Serve the noodles in bowls with chopsticks, scattered with the crispy garlic. Add some Thai basil flowers as a garnish, if you like.

SHARING

DISHES

MINCED PORK & CRAB LON WITH CUCUMBER

This simplified version of a traditional Thai dish called "lon", which is usually a simmered coconut cream "relish" served with raw or blanched vegetables to dip, such as long beans, cucumber, radishes, aubergine (eggplant) or green mango comes courtesy of Dan Turner, sous chef at Farang. Crispy pork and fish skins are also ideal accompaniments, as are herbs like Thai basil, sawtooth coriander and betel leaves.

Feeds 2 as a smaller plate. Gluten-free

250ml (9fl oz) coconut cream	25g (1oz) minced pork belly (at least 25% fat)	50g (1¾oz) crab meat (half white, half brown)	1 teaspoon palm sugar	juice of 1 lime, to taste	1 small shallot or small red onion, sliced	1 cucumber

Pour the coconut cream into a small saucepan and bring to the boil over a medium heat. Add the minced pork, stirring constantly to break up the meat, then reduce the heat and simmer for 2 minutes. Stir in the brown crab meat, the palm sugar and **1 teaspoon of fish sauce**. Cook until the palm sugar dissolves and the mixture has thickened, then stir in the white crab meat and turn off the heat.

Squeeze in a little lime juice to add some sourness to balance the rest of the dish, which is silky, rich and creamy with a salty edge and a sweet background. Serve in small bowls ready for dipping.

Slice **1 long red chilli** into 1cm (½in) thick slices or rings and sprinkle the desired amount on top of the relish/dip along with the shallot or red onion slices. Slice the cucumber lengthways in such a way as to allow each slice to be used as a spoon, and serve with the relish/dip.

WHOLE SPICED YELLOW CRAB CURRY

This delicious curry from Dan Turner, Sous chef at Farang, can also be enjoyed by vegetarians by replacing the crab with 200g (7oz) green beans, baby corn and broccoli and the fish sauce with soy sauce.

Feeds 2. Vegetarian, vegan (replace the egg with 1 tablespoon of cornflour dissolved in 100ml/3½fl oz cold water)

| 1 whole fresh crab (about 500g–600g/1lb 2oz–1lb 5oz) | 2cm (¾in) piece of turmeric | 2 onions, roughly sliced into large chunks | 250ml (9fl oz) coconut cream | 1 tablespoon mild curry powder | 1 tablespoon caster sugar | 2 eggs, cracked into a bowl |

First, dispatch the crab by putting it to sleep in the freezer for an hour. Alternatively, you can use frozen crab claws or 200g (7oz) pre-picked crab meat from your fishmonger.

Bring 10 litres (17½ pints) of water to the boil in a very large pot and add 35g (1½oz) of table salt, and if you have any scraps of lemongrass, galangal or kaffir lime leaf from other recipes, add them, too. Poach the crab for 12 minutes per 1kg (2lb 4oz). Prepare an ice bath and immediately after cooking, place the cooked crab in it.

Once cooled, remove from the water and drain. Twist off the legs and claws and set aside. Separate the body and the shell by pressing down with your palm on the body and getting your fingers between the gap where the body and shell meet – it will come away in one piece. Remove and discard the gills, as they are inedible. Scrape out the brown meat from the shell and save for later, then, using a large sharp knife, slice the body in two in one motion, so no tiny bits of shell are shattered off. Set aside for later.

At this point, you can either pre-crack the claws using crab crackers, or wrap them individually in a towel and hit gently but firmly with a pestle, leaving the majority of the shell on. Alternatively, you can start cooking the dish.

Make the paste by pounding the turmeric and **2 peeled garlic cloves** together using a pestle and mortar. Chop **1 long red chilli** and **1 long green chilli** roughly into 1cm (½in) pieces (if you prefer it less spicy, remove the seeds, or use deseeded red peppers).

Heat **2 tablespoons of vegetable oil** in a nonstick wok over a high heat until the oil begins to smoke. Add the onions and chillies, then stir and toss until they begin to char, then add the garlic and turmeric paste. Cook until the paste turns golden, then pour in the coconut cream and stir in the brown crab meat, curry powder, caster sugar and **2 tablespoons of fish sauce**. Simmer for a moment, then add the crab body, legs and claws and simmer over a low-medium heat for 2 minutes. Finally, stir in the eggs. Continue cooking and stirring until the eggs are cooked through and the coconut has thickened. Add more fish sauce or sugar to taste. Serve with lime wedges, if you like.

COAL-ROASTED SCALLOPS WITH NAHM YUM

This dish has people queuing round the block when I have cooked it in the past – it's simple, fresh and perfect to scale up when you have some mates round. Grilling scallops in the shell on the coals is visually attractive and tastes amazing as the smoky flavour from the coals imparts into the scallops. However, it is not necessary to cook them like this, you can just pan-fry the scallops and roast the shells in the oven to get a similar-looking dish without having to light up the barbecue. Be careful, though, as a scallop shell-shaped burn to your hands will stick with you for a while.

Feeds 2. Gluten-free

3 teaspoons caster sugar	juice of 3 limes	juice of 1 clementine	4 fresh scallops, opened, skirt removed (shells cleaned and reserved)	1 crunchy, sour dessert apple, cored and diced

Preheat the barbecue until hot.

Start by preparing the nahm yum dressing. Using a pestle and mortar, pound together **2 peeled garlic cloves** and **3 chopped long red chillies** (deseeded if you don't like too much heat) to make a coarse paste, using the caster sugar as an abrasive. Stir the lime juice, clementine juice and **3 tablespoons of fish sauce** into the paste, and then taste. The dressing should taste sweet, salty, spicy and sour in equal measure. If the taste is too much in one direction for you, then adjust accordingly by upping the other three flavours; the key is in the balance.

Using your hands, rub **a little vegetable oil** on to the shelled scallops and sprinkle with a little salt. Place the scallop shells, outer shell down, on to the red hot embers and leave for 30 seconds for the heat to penetrate. Gently place an oiled scallop into the centre of each shell – the scallop will sizzle as you put it down and it begins to fry on the shell. Fry for 1–1½ minutes and then turn each scallop over and fry on the other side for the same amount of time, cooking until both sides have turned golden brown. Once the scallops are cooked, remove the entire shells with the scallops from the heat and set aside to rest for 2 minutes.

To serve, arrange the scallops on a plate, then spoon over the nahm yum dressing, covering each scallop and leaving a little pool of dressing in the scallop shells. Finish by sprinkling the diced crunchy apple over them, then they are ready to eat. For more of a fill, serve with steamed jasmine rice.

STICKY TAMARIND & PALM SUGAR ROAST LOBSTER WITH SOUR APPLE

Melting fish sauce and palm sugar together creates a savoury caramel that I could happily eat with a spoon. It's especially delicious in this recipe when used to season the sweet meat of lobster. I roast the lobster in the oven here, but if you have a barbecue, grill it over wood and glaze it with the sauce during cooking. Lobster has an amazing way of absorbing the smoky flavour when grilled over open flame.

Feeds 2. Gluten-free

1 large lobster weighing 300–400g (10½–14oz), chopped in half down the centre, with the stomach sac and the intestines removed and discarded	2 tablespoons tamarind paste	100g (3½oz) palm sugar (or 50g/1¾oz caster sugar)	1 large sour dessert apple (such as Granny Smith), cored and diced	2 tablespoons chopped dill	1 lime, sliced into cheeks or wedges

Preheat the oven to 180°C/350°F/gas mark 4.

First, prepare the lobster. Pound **3 peeled garlic cloves** using a pestle and mortar, then add **3 tablespoons of fish sauce** and **3 tablespoons of vegetable oil** to the garlic and stir. Spoon this mix evenly over the lobster flesh and leave at room temperature for 10 minutes for the flavours to infuse.

Meanwhile, add the tamarind paste, sugar and **3 tablespoons of fish sauce** to a saucepan and gently melt. Once melted, simmer the sauce for 5 minutes until it is beginning to thicken, then remove from the heat.

Place the lobster halves, flesh-side up, on a nonstick roasting tray and roast on the middle shelf for 10 minutes. Remove from the oven and coat completely in the sauce, then return to the top shelf and roast for a further 5–6 minutes until the flesh has turned opaque, is hot throughout and comes away from the shell easily. Remove from the oven and leave to rest for a few minutes.

Place half a lobster on each plate and spoon over any leftover caramelized fish sauce from the tray. Sprinkle generously with the diced apple and dill, then serve with lime for squeezing and some sticky rice to mop up all the juices, if you wish.

GRILLED BABY SQUID WITH CHILLI OIL

In Thailand, grilled squid is known as "pla muek yang" and is the perfect roadside sharing food. Skewers of squid are roasted over open flame and purchased on the go, accompanied by dipping sauces in a bag.

Feeds 2. Gluten-free

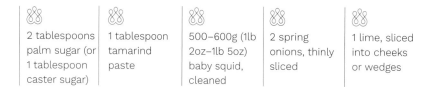

2 tablespoons palm sugar (or 1 tablespoon caster sugar)	1 tablespoon tamarind paste	500–600g (1lb 2oz–1lb 5oz) baby squid, cleaned	2 spring onions, thinly sliced	1 lime, sliced into cheeks or wedges

Preheat the barbecue to hot (if using a barbecue). Roughly chop **6 peeled garlic cloves** or pound them to a paste using a pestle and mortar.

Pour **300ml (½ pint) of vegetable oil** into a deep, heavy-based saucepan and heat over a medium heat to 180°C (350°F). To test if the temperature is correct, place a small amount of garlic in the hot oil and see how it reacts. It should bubble gently and float on the surface; if it sinks, it is not hot enough and if it spits and hisses, the oil is too hot.

Add all of the garlic to the hot oil and fry for 3–4 minutes until golden brown. Place a metal sieve over a heatproof bowl and carefully pour the oil and garlic through the sieve, then tease the garlic apart with a fork. Transfer the cooked garlic on to kitchen paper and leave to cool.

Repeat with **6 dried long red chillies (tops removed)**, using the same oil, they will take about a minute to darken. Set the residual oil to one side and leave to cool slightly.

To make the chilli oil, pound together the sugar, dried chillies, crispy garlic, tamarind paste and **2 tablespoons of fish sauce** using a pestle and mortar, then combine with 100ml (3½fl oz) of the residual oil. Have a little taste, it should be a subtle balance of smoky, spicy, sweet and salty, so adjust to suit your taste buds.

If not using a barbecue, preheat the grill to high or preheat a griddle pan over a high heat. Skewer the squid, gloss with a little of the chilli oil and either place over the hot barbecue, under the hot grill, or in the preheated griddle pan – they should sizzle as they touch the grill rack or griddle pan if it's hot enough. Cook for 2 minutes on each side until the squid has delicious golden-brown char lines on the outside of the flesh and is hot and tender throughout. Remove from the heat and rest for 2 minutes.

To serve, place the squid skewers on a long plate with bowls of the chilli oil alongside for dipping. Sprinkle with the spring onions and serve with the lime cheeks or wedges.

STEAMED SEABASS WITH GINGER & LIME

At Farang, we always have a whole seabass dish on the menu as it's such a lovely fish to eat. This recipe will work with any other whole white fish of a similar size. I use a steamer, but if you don't have one, not to worry, you can wrap the fish and the stock in a deep roasting tray, then cover and roast at 200°C/400°F/gas mark 6 for 13-15 minutes. This will not produce exactly the same results but will still be delicious.

Feeds 2-3. Gluten-free

| 1 whole seabass, about 250–300g (9–10½oz), scaled, cleaned and scored to the bone on both sides | 300ml (½ pint) fish stock | 20g (¾oz) ginger, peeled and chopped into rough matchsticks | 2 kaffir lime leaves, torn a little to release flavour | 8 cherry tomatoes | small handful of Thai basil leaves | 1 lime, sliced into cheeks or wedges |

First, set up your steamer and get the water boiling ready for action.

Season the fish and prepare the broth. Place the seabass in a lipped tray and spoon over **2 tablespoons of fish sauce**, massaging it all over the fish.

Select a second lipped tray, large enough to hold the fish, which also fits in the steamer. Add the stock, three-quarters of the ginger, the kaffir lime leaves, cherry tomatoes and **2 red or green bird's eye chillies**, nudged open a little using a pestle and mortar.

Lower the seabass into the stock as if you were putting it in the bath and then place it into the steamer. Steam on full for 13–15 minutes until the fish is white and hot to the bone, yet still moist. To check if the fish is ready, gently tease a little flesh from the bone using a spoon; when it lifts away from the bone with ease it is cooked. Once cooked, remove from the steamer and place to one side for a few minutes to leave the fish to cool slightly.

Using a large, lipped serving dish, capable of holding a little broth, place the seabass in the centre. Taste a little of the broth, it should be a little sweet from the tomatoes, a little salty from the fish sauce and spicy from the chilli, so if it is too spicy or salty for you, add a pinch of caster sugar to balance. Pour the broth (and flavourings) from the steamer over the seabass. Scatter heavily with the Thai basil and the remaining ginger, then serve with steamed jasmine rice and the lime cheeks or wedges for squeezing.

HOT-SMOKED SALMON WITH RUNNY DUCK EGGS & CHILLI BUTTER

This impressive crowd-pleaser is fantastic cooked on a barbecue as the added smokiness creates a delicious dish, but it can be cooked with ease in the oven, too.

Feeds 6-8. Gluten-free

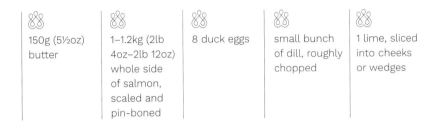

150g (5½oz) butter	1–1.2kg (2lb 4oz–2lb 12oz) whole side of salmon, scaled and pin-boned	8 duck eggs	small bunch of dill, roughly chopped	1 lime, sliced into cheeks or wedges

Gently melt the butter in a medium saucepan with **4 finely sliced long green and red chillies, peeled cloves from ½ head of garlic (roughly pounded using a pestle and mortar) and 4 tablespoons of fish sauce.** Using your hands and a tablespoon, carefully spoon the seasoned butter over the flesh side of the salmon while gently massaging it all over the flesh. Leave at room temperature for 30 minutes to let the flavours infuse.

Get the barbecue hot or preheat the oven to 200°C/400°F/gas mark 6. The salmon is best cooked fast over a high heat. Place the salmon in a roasting tray and cook over a barbecue or in the oven for 15–20 minutes. Test if it is cooked by teasing the flesh with a spoon, if it flakes easily and lifts away from the skin, and is hot throughout, it is ready. Remove from the heat and leave to rest for 5 minutes.

Meanwhile, cook the eggs. Bring a large saucepan of salted water to a gentle rolling boil, then carefully place the eggs into the water. Cook the eggs for 6½ minutes (or for 9 minutes if you don't like a runny yolk) and then remove and place them into iced water. To make them easy to peel, drop a splash of white vinegar into the iced water. As soon as the eggs are cool enough to handle, lift them out, one at a time, and, using the back of a tablespoon, gently crack the top and bottom of the egg and place back in the water – the vinegar water will do its magic, making the shell slide off with ease in your hand. Repeat until all the eggs are peeled. Slice the eggs in half, ready to serve.

Place the salmon on a large serving dish or banana leaf if you have any. Scatter the duck eggs around the salmon, runny-side up, with a tiny pinch of salt in each of the yolks. Sprinkle the dill over the salmon and drizzle over any excess fish sauce butter. Serve with sticky rice, lime cheeks or wedges and bowls of sriracha (hot chilli sauce) to add some extra spice, if you're into that kind of thing.

GRILLED SARDINES WITH CRISPY GARLIC, SHALLOTS & HERBS

This is a simple and quick dish to cook at home. I love using sardines, but this recipe is great with mackerel or other fish with a high natural oil content. Get the freshest fish you can and let it do the talking with this one, it's perfect for a sunny afternoon lunch. Try cooking the fish over a barbecue if you have one – it's delicious.

Feeds 2-3. Gluten-free

2 tablespoons peeled and roughly chopped turmeric	2 banana shallots, diced	200g (7oz) fresh sardines, gutted and cleaned	1 lime	handful of Thai basil leaves	handful of coriander leaves

To make the marinade, pound **6 peeled garlic cloves** with the turmeric and shallots to make a coarse paste using a pestle and mortar. Scrape this paste into a bowl and mix with **2 tablespoons of fish sauce** and **1 tablespoon of vegetable oil**, then use this mixture to coat the sardines completely. Once coated, place the sardines on a plate in the fridge and leave for 30 minutes to let all the flavours get to know each other.

Fire up a griddle pan over a high heat, then fry the sardines with all the marinade ingredients for 2 minutes on each side until the skins are golden brown. Ensure you move the marinade around often, too, so that all the ingredients cook evenly. Once the sardines are cooked, turn off the heat, remove the sardines to a plate and leave to rest for a few minutes.

Meanwhile, squeeze the lime juice into the griddle pan to pick up all the juices and leftover marinade, add another small squirt of fish sauce, stir, then spoon the contents back over the fish.

Top with the picked Thai basil and coriander leaves to serve. These are delicious as a light snack on their own or served with steamed jasmine rice.

WHOLE GRILLED MACKEREL "NAHM YUM"

Mackerel is one of my all-time favourite fish but for some reason, I have found that when mackerel is put on the menu it is not very popular with the general public. This is a real shame, so I am attempting to push it one step more by including it here. Mackerel is high in omega-3 fatty acids and is in the same family as tuna, sharing similar characteristics, such as a lack of scales, and a similar flavour from the rich, natural oils present in the flesh – a true ocean treat.

Feeds 2. Gluten-free

3 tablespoons palm sugar	juice of 2 limes	juice of 1 mandarin (or use 1 clementine or 1 small orange)	2 tablespoons Thai sticky rice, toasted (see page 73)	3 tablespoons tamarind paste	2 whole mackerel, each weighing about 250–300g (9–10½oz), cleaned and gutted, with bloodline removed	1 mandarin, sliced into cheeks or wedges (or use a clementine or a small orange)

Toast **6 dried long eye chillies** in a dry pan over a medium heat for 3–4 minutes until darkened slightly and crisp, then cool and pound to a powder using a pestle and mortar or a spice grinder (use more if you're hard enough, less if you're not).

To make the dressing, combine the palm sugar, **2 tablespoons of fish sauce**, the lime juice, half the mandarin juice, the toasted rice, dried chilli powder and tamarind paste using a pestle and mortar. It should be salty, smoky, a little sweet and nutty from the toasted rice, so adjust accordingly.

Heat either a griddle pan or a barbecue to a medium-high heat. Coat the mackerel in **2 tablespoons of vegetable oil** and sprinkle each with a pinch of salt, ensuring you rub it all around the fish. Place the fish on the hot griddle or grill rack and cook for 5–6 minutes on each side until the skin is golden brown and crispy and the inside is cooked through. Test the fish is cooked by pushing a metal skewer through the flesh, it should slide in with ease and come out piping hot. When you are happy the fish is cooked, remove from the heat and set aside to rest for 2 minutes.

Serve the fish on the centre of a plate and spoon over the dressing. Accompany with the mandarin cheeks or wedges for squeezing, alongside some steamed jasmine rice and garnished with Thai basil, coriander or dill, if you like.

LEMONGRASS-SKEWERED FISHCAKES

When buying your fish for these, ask your fishmonger to include a little smoked haddock in the mix, or if not available, ensure you have some wood chips, a colander and clingfilm for a quick home smoke technique. The smoked fish combined with the fresh red curry paste turns these into little spicy balls of smoky, fishy heaven. I use salmon and haddock in this recipe, but it works with a range of different fish. However, steer clear of using flat fish as the proteins do not break down enough and the texture is not right for the cakes. Spearing the fishcakes on a bruised stick of lemongrass makes for a great natural skewer and it imparts its delicious aroma into the fish mixture.

Feeds 4. Gluten-free

| 80g (2¾oz) palm sugar (or soft light brown sugar) | 80g (2¾oz) tamarind paste | 200g (7oz) salmon fillet, skinned, chopped into small chunks | 200g (7oz) haddock, skin and bloodline removed, chopped into small chunks | about 20g (¾oz) galangal, peeled and roughly chopped | 1 egg, beaten | 8 lemongrass stalks, lightly bruised with a pestle |

Slice **8 dried long red chillies** in half lengthways and remove the seeds, then soak in freshly boiled water for 2 hours to soften. Drain and set aside.

Gently melt the palm sugar and **80ml (3fl oz) of fish sauce** together in a small saucepan, being careful not to boil the mixture and caramelize the sugar. Stir in the tamarind paste, then set aside to cool.

Place the salmon and haddock in a colander. Pour 100g (3½oz) wood chips into a large saucepan and place over a high heat. Keep your eye on these and have a small bowl of water, the colander of fish and some clingfilm ready. Once the wood chips begin to alight, dip your fingers into the water and flick it on to the wood chips to put them out and create smoke. Remove the pan from the heat, then immediately place the colander of fish over the smoking chips and cover the whole lot with clingfilm as quickly as possible, enclosing the smoking wood embers and the fish within. Do this in a well-ventilated area. Leave for at least 30 minutes to allow the fish to take on the smoke. If you are not in a rush, place the home-made smoker in the fridge (once the pan has cooled down) and leave overnight for a more intense smoky flavour. Alternatively, you can skip this part if you like, as the fishcakes are still delicious unsmoked.

Pound the soaked red chillies to a paste using a pestle and mortar. Add the galangal and continue to pound, then finish with **4 peeled garlic cloves** and pound everything to a smooth paste. ——————>

Place the fish, chilli paste and cooled fish sauce and sugar mix in a food processor and blitz until well mixed. Scrape out into a mixing bowl, then stir in the beaten egg using your hands. Next, get an empty bowl, then pick up small handfuls of the fishcake mix from one bowl and throw it into the empty bowl with enough speed to make a slapping sound. Repeat this process 2–3 times so that the proteins in the fish come together and form a bouncy fishcake mix. Split the mix into eighths and shape each portion around a lemongrass stalk, shaping them tightly into elongated balls, leaving a little lemongrass sticking out of both ends so it is easy to pick up and eat. For best results, leave the fishcakes in the fridge for 30 minutes to set into shape, then gloss with a little vegetable oil before cooking.

These fishcakes taste best cooked over charcoal or wood, but if you don't have a barbecue, preheat the oven to 180°C/350°F/gas mark 4 and bake them on a baking tray for 20 minutes. To cook on the barbecue, use mainly charcoal with a little wood (charcoal for lasting heat and wood for smoke and flavour). Once the embers are glowing red to give a medium heat, place the skewers on the rack above the embers (they should lightly sizzle, but if the embers begin to smoke like a chimney, remove and wait for the heat to die down a bit). Cook the fishcakes for 15–20 minutes until hot throughout, turning them every 5 minutes. Once the fishcakes are golden brown, remove and leave to rest for 5 minutes.

The fishcakes are delicious eaten warm as they are. However, a few serving suggestions would be cheeks or wedges of lime, sweet chilli dipping sauce or fresh coriander leaves, or all three.

SALT-BAKED SEABASS WITH FRESH LIME

The first time I served this dish, I assumed that everyone had eaten salt-baked fish before, so a little advice: never assume anything. I poked my head out from the kitchen to see people munching down on blocks of roasted egg whites and salt, and although I found it quite funny, a few others were not joining me in laughter. For those of you new to the salt-bake game, it is a cooking method in which egg whites and salt are combined and used to encase an ingredient. When roasted, the mixture forms a hard casing around the ingredient, sealing in the flavour and allowing it to roast without drying out.

Feeds 3. Gluten-free

3 egg whites	500–600g (1lb 2oz–1lb 5oz) coarse rock salt	1 wild line-caught seabass, about 1.25kg (2lb 12oz), gutted but not scaled	2 lemongrass stalks, touch outer layer removed, bruised	4 kaffir lime leaves, torn to release flavour	1 lime, sliced into cheeks or wedges

Preheat the oven to 200°C/400°F/gas mark 6.

Line a nonstick baking tray, large enough to fit the fish on, with nonstick baking parchment. Next, whisk the egg whites in a bowl until soft peaks form, then mix with the coarse rock salt. Now you want to encase the fish in the salt mix to make an "oven". Put around a third of the salt mix on the lined baking tray, then lay the fish on top. Place the lemongrass and kaffir lime leaves on top of the fish. Spread the rest of the salt mix over the fish so it is covered entirely, leaving no gaps. It's a messy job, but use a spatula or the back of a spoon to spread the mix over. You can now leave it in the fridge for up to 2 hours or bake it straight away.

Roast on the middle shelf for 30–35 minutes to cook through. To check it is cooked, you should be able to insert a metal skewer through the hard crust and straight through the fish, if it slides through easily and comes out hot, you are in business.

To serve, break the crust – it will come off in big chunks. Then carefully, using a knife and fork, gently pull off the fish skin. Fillet the top layer of fish, remove the main bone and head, then take the rest of it off the bone. Do this at the table in front of guests for an impressive dinner party trick.

Serve with the lime cheeks or wedges and sticky rice. If you have time, accompany with a fresh nahm yum dressing (see page 24) on the side.

SWEET & SPICY STICKY PORK RIBS

Sticky pork ribs coated in sweet, spicy, soy-rich glaze are common all around Thailand. Serve them with crispy fried shallots and green papaya salad for a combination made in heaven – in fact, these are the dishes that originally made me fall for Thai cuisine.

Feeds 2–3

| 300ml (½ pint) kecap manis (sweet soy sauce) | 100g (3½oz) palm sugar (or 50g/1¾oz) caster sugar) | 1 lemongrass stalk, tough outer layer removed, the rest sliced as thinly as possible | 1 rack of pork ribs | 1 lime, cut into wedges | small handful of coriander leaves | small handful of mint, leaves torn in half |

Preheat the oven to 180°C/350°F/gas mark 4 (if cooking straight away).

Using a large granite pestle and mortar, pound together the kecap manis, sugar, lemongrass, **2 thinly sliced long red chillies**, **2 thinly sliced long green chillies** and **1 thinly sliced red or green bird's eye chilli** to form a coarse paste.

Coat the pork ribs in the marinade, using your hands to rub the paste all over the meat – I suggest wearing disposable gloves to do this. At this stage, if you have time, the meat can be placed in a dish and left to marinate in the fridge, ideally for 6 hours. However, if you are hungry and don't want to wait, put the ribs in a roasting tray and cover with foil, then roast for 1½–2 hours until the meat is tender and falling off the bone. The meat will still retain a little bite, but if you want the meat to melt in the mouth entirely, cook the ribs at 160°C/325°F/gas mark 3 for 3–4 hours instead.

If you are barbecuing, the ribs can be taken straight out of the oven and placed over a hot barbecue to colour, basting them regularly with the leftover marinade. If neither barbecuing nor smoking the ribs, chop/divide them into individual ribs, stack on a plate and garnish with the lime wedges, coriander and mint leaves. They are delicious served with some steamed jasmine rice.

SEARED FILLET STEAK WITH GREEN PEPPERCORN & COCONUT CREAM SAUCE

A pan-fried steak is not typically Thai. However, this version has a Thai accent and has been one of my favourite ways to eat steak for years now. This dish began as a stir-fry; we marinated the beef in sweet soy and then sealed the meat in a hot wok, finished it with the coconut and green peppercorn sauce and served it with jasmine rice – pretty tasty. Fresh green peppercorns can be hard to come by in a regular supermarket, but they are delicious, fragrant, spicy and well worth searching for; replace with dried black peppercorns if you can't find them.

Feeds 2

2 fillet steaks, roughly 4cm (1½in) thick, trimmed	4 tablespoons kecap manis	1 teaspoon fresh green peppercorns, picked from the stem	2 banana shallots, diced	500ml (18fl oz) coconut cream	1 heaped tablespoon rice flour	pinch of caster sugar (optional)

Coat the steaks with the kecap manis and a pinch of salt, rubbing it all in, then leave the steaks at room temperature for 30 minutes before cooking.

Meanwhile, prepare the sauce. Heat **2 tablespoons of vegetable oil** in a medium saucepan over a medium-high heat and sweat the green peppercorns, shallots and **3 finely chopped (or pounded) garlic cloves** in the oil, stirring frequently, until translucent and fragrant.

Deglaze the pan with **1 tablespoon of fish sauce**, then add the coconut cream and bring to a simmer, being careful not to boil the cream. In a small bowl, whisk together the rice flour with a ladleful of the simmering cream until it is smooth, then return to the pan and stir thoroughly to incorporate the mix into the coconut cream. Continue to simmer this very gently for a further 8–10 minutes, stirring occasionally, until the cream is thick and resembles the viscosity of a gravy. Give it a taste, it should be salty, savoury and peppery, but add a pinch of caster sugar if it's too salty for you.

Heat **2 tablespoons of vegetable oil** in a large frying pan over a high heat and when it's sizzling hot, add the steaks and fry for 5 minutes on each side for medium, 1 minute less on each side for rare, or 1 minute more on each side for well done. Remove to a plate, cover and set aside to rest in a warm place for 5 minutes before serving.

Serve the steaks with the thickened cream ladled on the side. Nice additions for garnish are matchsticks of peeled ginger, Thai basil leaves, sliced chillies or fresh coriander.

SPICED LAMB & EGG ROTI PARCELS

Here the trick is to cook the minced lamb filling an hour or so before you serve the dish, so that it has time to cool down. This way, all the flavours solidify together in the fat, allowing you to easily spoon the roti parcels full of the delicious, lightly spiced lamb. It's also tasty to throw a selection of chopped herbs through the minced lamb filling – Thai basil, coriander and mint make for excellent companions.

Feeds 4 (makes a little spare dough in case anything goes wrong)

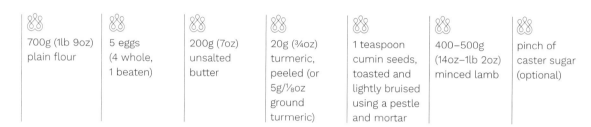

| 700g (1lb 9oz) plain flour | 5 eggs (4 whole, 1 beaten) | 200g (7oz) unsalted butter | 20g (¾oz) turmeric, peeled (or 5g/⅛oz ground turmeric) | 1 teaspoon cumin seeds, toasted and lightly bruised using a pestle and mortar | 400–500g (14oz–1lb 2oz) minced lamb | pinch of caster sugar (optional) |

To make the dough, sift the flour into a mixing bowl, make a well in the centre, then add the beaten egg, using a fork to mix them together. Add 350ml (12fl oz) of warm water, little by little, stirring with the fork until combined, then knead for 8–10 minutes. The dough should be tacky but not sticking to the bowl or your hand; if it's too wet, add a little flour; if it's too dry, add a little water. This dough is quite wet compared to regular bread dough. Place the dough in a lightly oiled bowl, then cover with clingfilm, ensuring the clingfilm is in direct contact with the dough to stop it crusting over, then leave to rest for a minimum of 30 minutes, but ideally a few hours, at room temperature.

Meanwhile, gently melt the butter in a small pan with half the fresh or ground turmeric. Once melted, you will see that the clarified butter has split from the solids. Pour the clarified (shiny and clear, not cloudy) butter gently into another container ready for use, and discard the fresh turmeric and the sediment at the bottom.

Next, make the spiced lamb filling. Heat 50g (1¾oz) of the clarified turmeric butter in a frying pan over a medium heat. Add the cumin seeds and **4 peeled garlic cloves (pounded using a pestle and mortar)** and gently roast in the butter for 2 minutes, stirring regularly, until the garlic turns a lovely golden-brown colour.

Add the minced lamb and continue to fry for a further 8–10 minutes until the lamb is cooked thoroughly and beginning to crisp a little in the bottom of the pan. Stir in **2 tablespoons of fish sauce** and taste (bear in mind the flavours should be big and bold as they also need to season the roti bread a little). If you feel it's too salty for your liking, add a pinch of caster sugar to bring back the balance a little. Remove from the heat and leave to cool for 1 hour before making the roti.

Now for the fun bit, cooking the roti. If you're feeling lucky, then try the traditional method by slapping out the roti dough. Lightly oil a clean surface. Form a small ball of dough by pulling off a chunk roughly the size of a golf ball. Repeat this until all the dough is in portion-sized balls (you will have more than the four balls you need, allowing spare dough if anything goes wrong).

Place a dough ball on the oiled surface. Flatten it into a rough circle and gently lift the side closest to you and drag it towards you, then lift it quickly but delicately and slap it back on to the surface (the elasticity and stickiness of the dough means that it doesn't rip too easily and it stretches bigger as you drag it). Repeat until the dough is roughly 2–3mm (1/16–1/8in) thick (the thinner the better, and a few holes are fine). Alternatively, you can use a rolling pin, or just stretch it out with your hands. It's hard to get it perfect the first time, so don't worry if it all goes a little pear-shaped, it will still taste amazing. Repeat to make three more decent rotis (any left over can be used to patch up any holes you have, see Tip page 55).

Heat 30g (1oz) clarified turmeric butter in a large frying pan over a medium heat (the butter needs to be hot to crisp the dough, but not burnt). Delicately lift a piece of dough into the pan; if it sizzles, you're doing it right. Immediately place a quarter of the spiced lamb mix in the centre of the roti, make a little well in the middle and crack an egg into it, then fold in all four sides like wrapping a parcel, encasing the filling and egg inside. Fry gently for 1–2 minutes until the underside is lovely and golden brown. Gently flip the roti parcel over and fry the underside for a further 2 minutes until golden brown and crispy, adding a little more butter whenever the pan becomes dry. Remove to a tray lined with kitchen paper to drain off any excess butter, while you assemble and cook the remaining roti parcels in the same way.

Eat the warm roti parcels, chopped into triangles, with your hands. They will taste savoury and delicious, and if you get the timings right, the egg should still be a little gooey in the middle. A little squirt of sriracha (hot chilli sauce) on the plate for dipping always goes down a treat.

CRYING TIGER BEEF NOODLES

I have no idea where the name of this dish comes from, but perhaps it's because the amount of dried chilli the recipe traditionally uses can seriously mess you up. I've also heard people call it "waterfall beef", describing how the juices that flow from the beef like a waterfall are used as part of the dressing.

Feeds 2. Gluten-free

150g (5½oz) dried flat rice noodles	2 tablespoons dry sticky rice, toasted and ground to a powder	3 tablespoons palm sugar	juice of 2 limes	3 tablespoons tamarind paste	200–300g (7–10½oz) beef steak, bavette or onglet	4 big chunks of Iceberg lettuce

Put the rice noodles in a bowl, cover with boiling water and leave for 8–10 minutes to soften, stirring occasionally. Drain, refresh in cold water, drain again and set aside.

Roast **6 dried long red bird's eye chillies** in a dry frying pan over a medium heat for about 3 minutes, stirring constantly, until they darken and smoke a little. Leave to cool and pound to a powder using a pestle and mortar or a spice grinder.

Using a pestle and mortar, grind together the palm sugar, **2 tablespoons of fish sauce**, the lime juice, toasted sticky rice, chilli powder and tamarind paste until combined. It should be salty, smoky, a little sweet and nutty from the roasted rice. Set aside.

Coat the steak in **a few tablespoons of vegetable oil**, sprinkle with a pinch of sea salt and massage it into the flesh, then allow the meat to get to room temperature before cooking. In a very hot frying pan or griddle pan or under a preheated grill, cook the steak; it is important for the steak to be quite rare to retain as much blood and flavour as possible to mix with the dressing. I cook it for 2–3 minutes on either side, depending on the thickness of the steak, then wrap it in clingfilm to retain moisture and leave it to rest for 5 minutes in a warm place. Then slice it across the grain into bite-sized pieces, roughly 1cm (½in) thick.

Tip the steak and all the juices on the chopping board into a mixing bowl, add the dressing and the rice noodles, then toss and stir thoroughly, ensuring all the noodles have been coated and seasoned. Plate the noodles on the Iceberg lettuce leaves in neat piles. The lettuce adds a welcome fresh crunch to this otherwise soft dish. Garnish with an extra sprinkle of toasted rice powder, if you have it, for added texture, then serve with chopsticks and napkins to mop up the "tears".

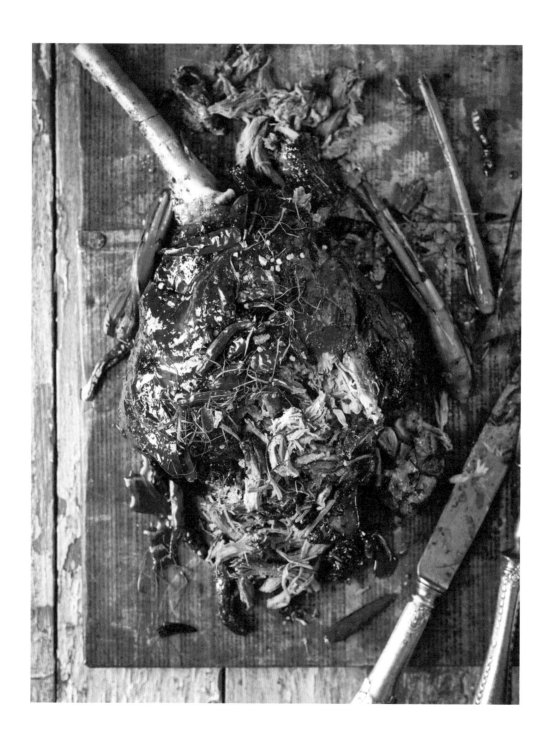

ROAST LAMB SHOULDER WITH FERMENTED SHRIMP GLAZE

The lamb in this popular wedding dish ends up so tender that diners can serve themselves the meat using nothing but a tablespoon. It's delicious accompanied by the chilli, galangal and mint sauce (see page 136).

Feeds 5–6. Gluten-free

50g (1¾oz) fermented shrimp paste	3kg (6lb 8oz) lamb shoulder on the bone	8 kaffir lime leaves, torn to release flavour	4 lemongrass stalks, bruised	about 40g (1½oz) galangal, bruised	2 onions, roughly chopped	500g (1lb 2oz) palm sugar

Preheat the oven to 200°C/400°F/gas mark 6. Wrap the fermented shrimp paste in foil and roast for 10 minutes. Remove and set aside.

Roast **12 dried long red chillies** in a dry frying pan over a medium heat for about 3 minutes, stirring constantly, until they darken and smoke a little. Set aside to cool, then crush or lightly pound into flakes.

In a large boiling pan, submerge the lamb shoulder in water and then add **2 sliced heads of garlic**, the kaffir lime leaves, lemongrass, galangal, onions, a big pinch of salt and 200g (7oz) of the palm sugar. Cover the surface with a circle of nonstick baking parchment and the lid and bring to a simmer. Cook for 4–5 hours, or until nearly falling off the bone. Remove the lamb from the pot and set aside on a plate. Reserve the stock for later.

Meanwhile, make the glaze. Add the remaining palm sugar to a saucepan with **100ml (3½fl oz) of fish sauce** and the roasted shrimp paste. Cook over a medium heat, stirring occasionally, until all there are no lumps. Simmer the paste for 10 minutes until it is thick enough to paint on to a piece of meat with a brush.

Reduce the oven temperature to 180°C/350°F/gas mark 4. Put the lamb in a nonstick roasting tray, transfer this to the middle shelf of the oven and roast for 25–30 minutes until the meat starts to crisp a little. Paint on a thick coating of the glaze, then return to the oven for a further 10 minutes until the sugar has caramelized on the meat.

Meanwhile, strain the reserved stock into a clean saucepan, then add any leftover glaze. Bring to the boil, then simmer for 30–40 minutes, skimming the fat and discarding it regularly. Once the fat stops collecting on the surface, it is ready.

Serve the lamb shoulder whole as a centrepiece, coated with the crispy dried chillies and stock for pouring over. Accompany with steamed jasmine rice and a nice salad.

SIRLOIN STEAK WITH ROASTED CHILLI RELISH

This relish is best made over an open fire or on a barbecue to give it a delicious smoky flavour. If you don't have a barbecue, try charring the vegetables over a gas flame before roasting and softening them in the oven. It's best to skewer the vegetables and lightly coat them in oil so that you can cook large amounts at the same time.

Feeds 2. Gluten-free

4 banana shallots, unpeeled	10 cherry tomatoes	2 lemongrass stalks, ends trimmed	2 sirloin steaks	1 tablespoon palm sugar (or light soft brown sugar)	juice of ½ lime

Skewer the shallots, cherry tomatoes, lemongrass, **8 large red chillies** and **2 green bird's eye chillies** ready for cooking.

Light the barbecue. Lightly coat each prepared skewer and **half a head of garlic (cut in half widthways)** with **vegetable oil**. Place all the skewers and garlic over a high heat, turning them regularly to ensure even cooking, until the vegetables are softened, cooked and lightly charred. This can be replicated by roasting the skewers on a baking tray in a preheated oven at 180°C/350°F/gas mark 4 for about 30 minutes, if you prefer.

Meanwhile, remove the steaks from the fridge 30 minutes before cooking to bring them to room temperature.

Once cooked, remove all the vegetables and spices from the skewers and set aside until they are cool enough to handle. Next, remove all the chilli stems and cores and the garlic and shallot skins, then peel off the tough outer layers of the lemongrass and chop the remainder into small pieces. Add all of this to a food processor (or use a large pestle and mortar) with the palm sugar and about **1 tablespoon of fish sauce** and blitz (or pound) together to make a moist, coarse paste. Add the lime juice and check for seasoning, it should be smoky, spicy, salty and sour.

Whilst the barbecue is still nice and hot, cook the steaks. Gloss them with a little **vegetable oil** and a sprinkle of salt, then grill the steaks over the barbecue (or under a preheated hot grill if you don't have a barbecue) until they are cooked to your liking. I cook mine rare for about 3 minutes on each side and then rest them for 5 minutes.

Serve the steaks sliced into bite-sized chunks, with generous helpings of the roasted chilli relish to dunk the steak into.

BRAISED BEEF, GINGER & THAI BASIL RICE PORRIDGE

Otherwise known as "congee", or slightly less attractively, "gruel", this dish is a perfect brunch or dinner when you are feeding a hungry crowd. It's filling, comforting and, most importantly, really tasty. Congee is also something special made with smoked fish or mushrooms instead of beef. It may be gruel to some, but it tastes like heaven to me.

Feeds 2–3. Gluten-free (use gluten-free soy sauce)

250g (9oz) piece of beef shin (or any other cut for slow cooking)	roughly 40g (1½oz) ginger, peeled, half chopped into matchsticks, the other half left whole	small handful of Thai basil, leaves picked from stems, and stems reserved	300g (10½oz) broken jasmine rice (or wholegrain jasmine rice)	1 teaspoon ground white peppercorns	2 tablespoons light soy sauce	2 spring onions, finely sliced

Place the beef in a large pot and submerge in water with a pinch of salt, the whole piece of ginger, **4 peeled garlic cloves (pounded to a paste using a pestle and mortar)** and the Thai basil stems. Put the lid on and simmer gently for 3½–4 hours, or until the meat is soft and juicy. It should be so tender that you can push a spoon all the way through it. When ready, remove the meat from the stock and set aside until it's cool enough to handle, then chop it into spoon-sized chunks. Leave the stock to cool.

Strain the cooled braising liquid from the beef through a sieve to remove all solids. Measure out 1.25 litres (generous 2 pints) of the stock and pour into a large, nonstick pan. Add the rice to this, along with the ground white pepper, **1 tablespoon of fish sauce** and the soy sauce, then bring to a gentle simmer and put the lid on. Cook for 30–40 minutes, stirring every 5 minutes or so to ensure even cooking and no sticking, until the rice is soft and mushy and has absorbed most of the liquid – it should be almost a risotto consistency. Add the beef, half the ginger matchsticks and Thai basil leaves, and a touch more stock, if needed, and bring back up to a simmer.

Serve in bowls with the remaining chopped ginger, spring onions and some Thai basil flowers on top, if you have some. Mix **4 sliced red bird's eye chillies** with **4 tablespoons of fish sauce** in a ramekin and serve at the table, so people can add more seasoning as they wish.

BRAISED BEEF CLAY POT CURRY

Clay pots are perfect for cooking over a high heat as the food loses little to no moisture because it is surrounded by steam, creating a tender, flavourful dish. If you don't have a clay pot, you can use a roasting tray as below.

Feeds 2. Gluten-free

400g (14oz) beef cheeks, excess fat removed, chopped into 3cm (1¼in) chunks	2 lemongrass stalks, bruised using a pestle and mortar	4 kaffir lime leaves, torn to release flavour	600–700ml (20fl oz–1¼ pints) coconut cream	1 heaped tablespoon light soft brown sugar	20g (¾oz) Thai basil leaves

Coat the beef in **50ml (2fl oz) of vegetable oil** and 1 tablespoon of coarse sea salt, mixing well with your hands and ensuring that all the meat gets a good coating of oil and salt.

Light up a kettle barbecue (ie one with a domed lid) – for best results, lightly smoke the beef cheeks over wood. To do this, ignite some wood and allow it to burn until it begins to combust and turn black. Place the beef cheeks on the hot grill, above the wood, and flick a little water on to the wood to create smoke. Close the barbecue lid and smoke for 10 minutes. Open the barbecue lid, turn the cheeks over and then close again for a further 10 minutes. At this point, the beef should be a little charred on either side, smoky and ready to be slow-cooked, so remove it from the barbecue and set aside. If you don't have a barbecue, this can all be replicated in a large pan on the hob, if you like.

Preheat the oven to 140°C/275°F/gas mark 1.

Add the smoked beef cheeks, lemongrass, kaffir lime leaves, **2 long red chillies (bruised using a pestle and mortar), 1 head of garlic (sliced in half through the middle)**, the coconut cream, **4–5 teaspoons of fish sauce** and the sugar to a large roasting tray, then tightly wrap the tray in foil. Place on the middle shelf in the oven and cook for 4–5 hours.

Remove the beef from the oven and check that it is really tender; you should be able to break up a piece of meat with a spoon.

Once the beef is ready, taste the broth, it should be delicately sweet from the coconut cream with a moreish saltiness from the fish sauce, so add a little more of either if you think it necessary, then stir in all the Thai basil. Serve in bowls topped with some Thai basil flowers, if you have some to hand, acoompanied by steamed jasmine rice.

LAMB CHOPS WITH SMOKY HERITAGE TOMATO RELISH

Grill the chops using cherry wood on the barbecue for added flavour. I couldn't resist using heritage tomatoes for their colour and flavour, but you can use any mixture of tomatoes; beef tomatoes add a deliciously rich taste. The relish makes more than you'll need, but it keeps well in the fridge for up to 3 months (unopened).

Feeds 2. Gluten-free

2 banana shallots, unpeeled	500g (1lb 2oz) mixed heritage tomatoes	3 tablespoons tamarind paste	2 tablespoons palm sugar (or dark soft brown sugar)	4 lamb chops	2 tablespoons butter, softened	1 lime, sliced into cheeks or wedges

Preheat the oven to 180°C/350°F/gas mark 4.

Put **2 long red chillies**, **2 long green chillies**, the banana shallots, tomatoes and **½ head of garlic (broken into cloves but not peeled)** on a nonstick roasting tray. Drizzle with **vegetable oil** and sprinkle with ½ teaspoon of salt, then roast until each ingredient is slightly charred and soft within – about 20 minutes usually does the job.

Once all the ingredients are softened, remove from the oven and cool slightly, then peel the garlic cloves and shallots and discard any tomato vines and chilli stalks. Pound all the ingredients together using a large pestle and mortar (or you can use a food processor here, but I prefer it chunky), along with **3 tablespoons of fish sauce**, the tamarind paste and palm sugar. Taste it – the relish should be smoky, sour, spicy and savoury.

Coat the lamb chops in the softened butter and sprinkle with salt, then rub it in with your hands. Heat a frying pan over a medium heat, drizzle **a glug of vegetable oil** into the pan and fry the chops for 5–6 minutes on each side until the meat is hot and cooked through to the bone. I like to keep it a little pink for better flavour. Once cooked to your liking, remove the chops to a plate and leave to rest for 2 minutes.

Serve the chops piled up in the centre of a plate and spoon over some relish. Scatter over some fresh coriander, if you like, and serve with the lime cheeks or wedges for squeezing and sticky rice to eat with your hands.

TIP
The relish will keep in an airtight container in the fridge, but it will need re-seasoning with a little fresh lime juice before use, as the flavour goes flat in the fridge over time. If you want to keep the relish for longer, store it (once freshly made) in sealed, sterilized jars in the fridge for up to 3 months.

"MU PING", MARINATED PORK SKEWERS WITH DARK SOY & WHITE PEPPER

This sweet, smoky and easy street food dish is served almost everywhere in Thailand. Traditional recipes are even simpler than this one, but the addition of the chilli and the sesame oil in Dan Turner's version is very pleasing to the palate.

Feeds 8–10

600g (1lb 5oz) pork neck, sliced into 2–3cm (¾–1¼in) thick slices	100g (3½oz) pork fat, sliced into 1cm (½in) thick squares	1 teaspoon peeled and chopped galangal	3 tablespoons palm sugar	1 tablespoon dark soy sauce	1 teaspoon sesame oil	1 teaspoon ground white pepper

You will need 16–20 wooden or bamboo skewers; soak them in water for at least 10 minutes before threading the pork. Thread the pork strips on to the soaked (drained) skewers with a fat square every other strip. The fat will render during the cooking process and keep the meat moist.

To make the marinade, pound together **1 tablespoon of chopped garlic**, the galangal and **2 red or green bird's eye chillies** using a pestle and mortar (if you prefer it non-spicy, leave out the chillies), then pound in the palm sugar (or just chop and crush all these ingredients with a knife). Stir in the soy sauce, **4 tablespoons of fish sauce** and the sesame oil, then add the white pepper. Pour the marinade over the pork skewers and massage it in, if necessary. Cover and chill for at least 4 hours or overnight.

Fire up a charcoal barbecue and after 40 minutes–1 hour, the glowing embers should be ready to cook (the heat needs to be just right, otherwise the sugar will burn). Try placing your palm over the heat, if you can hold it there for more than 10 seconds, the heat is not enough, only 1 second and it is too hot. If you have some wooden smoking chips, they would also be handy, but neither they nor the barbecue are essential, as an electric grill or griddle pan on the hob will also work.

Cook the skewers for 5 minutes on each side until the meat has browned on the outside and is piping hot throughout. Serve immediately either on their own or with a nahm yum dressing (see page 24) and some sticky rice.

"GAI YANG", MARINATED BARBECUE CHICKEN

Sweet, salty, spicy grilled chicken is a common Thai street food snack. This recipe from Kev Mac, Farang chef, shows how to brine the meat before cooking. Soaking the chicken in this salt solution allows it to hold more liquid, resulting in juicy and delicious meat.

Feeds 4. Gluten-free

100g (3½oz) table salt	50g (1¾oz) soft brown sugar, plus 2 tablespoons for the marinade	1.5–2kg (3lb 5oz–4lb 8oz) spatchcocked chicken	1 tablespoon peeled and chopped turmeric	1 teaspoon ground white peppercorns	1 teaspoon coriander seeds, lightly toasted in a dry pan	2 tablespoons oyster sauce

To make the brine, add 1 litre (1¾ pints) of water, the table salt and the 50g (1¾oz) sugar to a saucepan over a medium heat, stirring occasionally until the salt and sugar are fully dissolved. Leave the brine to cool, then submerge the chicken in it and transfer to the fridge for 4 hours.

In a pestle and mortar, pound **4 peeled garlic cloves**, the turmeric and white pepper to a coarse paste. Add the coriander seeds, oyster sauce, **2 tablespoons of fish sauce** and 2 tablespoons of sugar (or you can also use honey instead) and combine using the pestle to grind the marinade together. It should be sweet and salty; add a little more sugar if you have a sweet tooth. Smother the spatchcocked chicken completely in the marinade. Wrap in clingfilm and chill in the fridge for 2 hours.

Either light the barbecue to a medium grilling heat or preheat the oven to 180°C/350°F/ gas mark 4. If barbecuing, place the chicken bone side down and leave to seal for 10–15 minutes. When golden brown on the cooking side, flip the chicken skin side down and cook for a further 10–25 minutes until the skin is crispy and golden brown. Baste the meat in the residual marinade towards the end of cooking.

If cooking in the oven, place the chicken on a baking tray skin side up and roast for 40–45 minutes until golden brown and crispy, baste in the residual marinade towards the end of cooking. You can test when the chicken is cooked either with a meat thermometer or by checking the colour of the flesh. If you have a probe, insert it into the chicken leg. If the temperature is 70°C (160°F) or above, remove from the heat, rest for 5 minutes and then serve. If you don't have a probe, make an incision right through to the leg bone and make sure the meat is no longer pink and the juices are running clear.

Chop the chicken into 8 pieces, distributing the white and the dark meat evenly. Serve with sticky rice, if you wish, and a sweet, sour and spicy salad or dipping sauce, such as the "Nahm Phrik Num" (see page 135).

CHICKEN & HERB STUFFED LEMONGRASS STALKS

Known as "ua si khai" in Thai, which literally translates as stuffed lemongrass, this recipe calls for the lemongrass parcels to be deep-fried in hot oil straight away. If, however, you have time, they are something else when smoked a little on the barbecue first.

Feeds 2-3. Gluten-free

20g (¾oz) ginger, peeled and roughly chopped	20g (¾oz) palm sugar (or light soft brown sugar)	250g (9oz) minced chicken	small handful of coriander, roughly chopped	4–6 lemongrass stalks, tough outer layer removed	1 egg, beaten

Using a large pestle and mortar, pound together **4 peeled garlic cloves, 1 roughly chopped long red chilli** and the ginger to make a coarse paste. Add the palm sugar and 1 tablespoon of fish sauce and pound until there are no lumps. Add the chicken and continue to pound until everything is combined – this means that the meat will cook in one piece, like a burger, rather than crumble when cooked. Fold in the coriander.

Using a sharp knife, make a slit 1cm (½in) in from the base of each lemongrass stalk and cut lengthways along the whole stem for 5–7.5cm (2–3in), then rotate the stalk 90 degrees and repeat. Repeat this a few times around the stem, and you will notice as you are slicing that each incision allows the lemongrass to be opened, creating a lemongrass "cage". (Warming the lemongrass slightly can help to make them pliable, so if you are having trouble, place in a steamer or covered in a microwave and heat for 2 minutes.) Using your fingers, place a quarter of the chicken filling into each lemongrass "cage".

Heat **700ml (1¼ pints) of vegetable oil** in a deep, heavy-based pan over a medium heat to 190°C (375°F). If you do not have a thermometer, then test the oil by putting a thin slice of lemongrass into the oil to see how it reacts. It should bubble gently and float on the surface, turning golden brown after about 1 minute. One at a time, dip each lemongrass "cage" into the beaten egg, covering the all of the meat, and then place into the hot oil, leaving the thin stalk sticking out of the pan. Fry for 3–4 minutes until golden brown and hot throughout. Check them by inserting a metal skewer into the centre of the meat and testing the temperature with your finger (it should immediately feel hot), or use a meat thermometer – you want the internal temperature to be above 78°C (172°CF). Remove to a wire rack placed over a tray/plate to allow any excess oil to run off.

Serve these hot and ready to eat with your hands. They are delicious on their own, or accompanied with salad, such as the "Som Tam" Salad (see page 41) or Pomelo Salad (see page 39), rice and dipping sauces.

SATAY ROASTED CHICKEN

Satay is commonly eaten across Asia and is traditionally used to marinate meat or vegetables before skewering and barbecuing over an open flame. If you make this satay chicken, you will never order satay chicken in a Thai joint ever again, as you might as well stay at home and make a better version yourself.

Feeds 4. Gluten-free

40g (1½oz) ginger, peeled	6 banana shallots, peeled	80g (2¾oz) roasted peanuts	80g (2¾oz) desiccated coconut	2 tablespoons palm sugar	500ml (18fl oz) coconut cream	1 large chicken, about 1.5kg (3lb 5oz)

Chop **8 large dried red chillies** in half with scissors, then soak in freshly boiled water for 20 minutes to soften. Drain and deseed.

Using a large pestle and mortar, pound the following ingredients, one at a time, until each begins to resemble a paste: the soaked chillies, ginger, **5 peeled garlic cloves**, the shallots, the peanuts and finally the coconut, using a pinch of salt with each as an abrasive, if needed. Return all the ingredients to the mortar and pound together until they become one paste. This paste will keep for a week or so in an airtight container in the fridge, or it can be frozen for up to 3 months.

Heat **6 tablespoons of vegetable oil** in a large, nonstick pan over a medium heat until hot. Add the paste and cook, using a spatula to scrape the paste as it will stick to the pan. Continue to fry for 15–20 minutes until the paste darkens slightly. Add the palm sugar, reduce the heat to medium, and continue to stir until the sugar caramelizes. Add **2 tablespoons of fish sauce** to deglaze any paste that has stuck to the pan. Remove from the heat, add the coconut cream and mix well, then set aside to cool.

Place the chicken in a tray and cover completely with all of the satay paste. Cover and leave to marinate in the fridge for a minimum of 2 hours, ideally overnight.

Preheat the oven to 200°C/400°F/gas mark 6. Place the marinated chicken, breast-side up, in a nonstick roasting tray, cover with foil, then roast on the middle shelf for 45 minutes–1 hour, removing the foil for the final 10 minutes of cooking. The paste should be beginning to crisp a little and the chicken juices should be running into the paste. Test that the chicken is cooked by making an incision right the way through to the leg bone and check if there are any signs of blood. If there are, then return it to the oven for 5–10 minutes. For best results, insert a meat thermometer – it should measure 75°C (167°F) when cooked. Set aside to rest for 5 minutes.

Carve the chicken at the table and serve with steamed jasmine rice.

CRISPY AUBERGINES WITH SOY & SESAME GLAZE

For best results with this dish, get yourself to an Asian supermarket and buy some Thai purple aubergines, they are brighter purple in colour, thinner and sweeter in taste than their Mediterranean counterpart. The dish is also tasty when made using Mediterranean ones, but I find the seeds a little bitter, so when preparing those aubergines, try to chop out the core a little so as not to include all the seeds.

Feeds 2. Vegetarian, vegan, gluten-free

300g (10½oz) rice flour or cornflour	2 aubergines, stems removed, chopped into bite-sized pieces	2 kaffir lime leaves, torn a little to release flavour	50ml (2fl oz) light soy sauce	1 tablespoon kecap manis	small handful of mint leaves	1 teaspoon toasted white sesame seeds

Tip the rice flour or cornflour into a tray and toss the aubergine pieces with the flour until thoroughly coated.

Pour **500ml (18fl oz) of vegetable oil** into a nonstick wok and heat over a medium heat to 180°C (350°F). To test the temperature of the oil, place a piece of aubergine in the hot oil and see how it reacts. It should bubble gently and float on the surface, turning golden brown and crispy after about 1 minute; if it sinks, the oil is not hot enough and if it burns within a minute, the oil is too hot, so adjust accordingly.

Line a separate tray with kitchen paper. Deep-fry the aubergine for 2–3 minutes until golden brown. Using a slotted spoon, remove each batch to the lined tray to drain off the excess oil. Repeat until all the aubergine pieces are cooked. Carefully strain the hot oil into a heat-resistant container and set aside; this can be recycled and used again in the future. Wipe out the wok.

To make the glaze, heat the wok over a low heat until hot, then add 100ml (3½fl oz) water, the soy sauce and kecap manis and stir until all ingredients have melted. Stir 1 teaspoon of the leftover rice flour or cornflour into the mix, reduce the heat to low and simmer the sauce to cook out the flour, it should turn thick and glossy (if it is too thick, add a little more stock). Now taste; it should be sweet and salty.

Return the fried aubergines to the wok and toss them through the glaze. Remove from the heat and garnish with the mint leaves. Serve with the sesame seeds sprinkled over the top, accompanied by steamed jasmine rice, if you wish.

KING OYSTER MUSHROOM CURRY

This is my "in 7" version of a mushroom yellow curry, not an easy task as most Thai curries have 15–20 ingredients in the paste alone, but I've managed it and it's delicious.

Feeds 2. Vegetarian, vegan

3 banana shallots, unpeeled	3 tablespoons peeled and sliced ginger	1 tablespoon peeled and roughly chopped turmeric	1 tablespoon mild curry powder	6 king oyster mushrooms, sliced into 2cm (¾in) chunks	2 tablespoons light soy sauce	300ml (½ pint) coconut cream

Begin by roasting the necessary ingredients – this can be done over a barbecue or in the oven. Smoking the ingredients over wood will give the paste an intense flavoursome finish, but cooking them in the oven is still delicious. If using the oven, preheat it to 180°C/350°F/gas mark 4.

Place **6 unpeeled garlic cloves, 4–5 finely diced long red chillies** and the shallots on a baking tray and roast for 25–30 minutes until they are softened and fragrant. Remove from the oven and leave until cool enough to handle, then peel the garlic and shallots.

Using a pestle and mortar, begin by pounding the toughest ingredients into a paste first, in this case it will be the ginger. Scrape the pounded ginger into a bowl, then do the same with the turmeric, roasted shallots, garlic and chillies. Once all these ingredients have been pounded into a paste, pound them together with the mild curry powder until combined to make an orange/yellow-coloured paste. This will keep in an airtight container in the fridge for up to 2 weeks; it will then begin to discolour, but will still be usable for another week or two.

Heat **4 tablespoons of vegetable oil** in a large, nonstick pan over a medium heat. Add the paste (it should sizzle on impact if the pan is hot enough), then fry for 10 minutes, stirring constantly and scraping to ensure that it does not stick to the pan, until it begins to darken slightly and the ingredients give off a lovely aroma.

When the flavours begin to come together, add the mushrooms and fry for a few minutes until the mushrooms start to brown a little on the surface. Deglaze the pan with the soy sauce, then stir in 200ml (7fl oz) of water and the coconut cream and simmer gently for 10–15 minutes.

Serve in bowls, sprinkled with fresh herbs, if you like, and some steamed jasmine rice alongside.

CURRIED ROAST PUMPKIN

This dish uses a simplified version of a green curry paste. I have chosen pumpkin as the filler but, to be honest, any squash you like may be used and also sweet potato or a mix of both are great additions to the curry. It may seem daunting to make a paste from scratch, but there is nothing more satisfying than chowing down on a feast of your own efforts, ingredients combined by brute force.

Feeds 2. Vegetarian, vegan, gluten-free (use seaweed sauce or gluten-free soy sauce)

2 lemongrass stalks, tough outer layer removed and ends trimmed, thinly sliced	2 tablespoons peeled and finely chopped galangal	3 banana shallots, diced	20g (¾oz) turmeric, peeled and roughly chopped	500g (1lb 2oz) pumpkin, deseeded and sliced into segments	2 tablespoons light soy sauce	400ml (14fl oz) coconut milk

Using a pestle and mortar, begin by pounding the toughest ingredients into a paste first, so the lemongrass and galangal, using a little coarse salt as an abrasive. Next, pound **4 long green chillies (halved and deseeded)**, the shallots, **6 peeled garlic cloves** and the turmeric. Return all the pounded ingredients to the mortar and pound together until everything comes together as one vibrant green paste. This paste will keep in an airtight container in the fridge for up to 2 weeks; it will then begin to discolour, but will still be usable for another week at the very least.

Preheat the oven to 180°C/350°F/gas mark 4.

Heat **3 tablespoons of vegetable oil** in a large, nonstick pan over a medium heat until hot, then add the paste – it should sizzle as it enters the pan. Fry the paste for 10 minutes, stirring and scraping constantly to ensure that it does not stick, until it begins to darken slightly and the ingredients give off a lovely aroma. When the flavours begin to come together, add the pumpkin and fry for a further few minutes until it starts to brown a little on the surface.

Deglaze the pan with the soy sauce and then let it out with 100ml (3½fl oz) of water and the coconut cream. Bring to a simmer and then taste. It should be sweet and salty with a gentle spice, so adjust as necessary. Pour this mix into a lipped, nonstick baking tray or shallow roasting tin and place on the middle shelf of the oven for 25–30 minutes until the pumpkin is soft and the curry has thickened.

Serve the curry in bowls with steamed jasmine rice, scattered with coriander or Thai basil leaves, if you like.

SAUCES, RELISHES & PICKLES

"NAHM PHRIK NUM", ROASTED CHILLI DIPPING SAUCE

Translating quite literally as "water chilli", "nahm phrik" essentially means an assortment of ingredients that are prepared and then pounded using a pestle and mortar to make a relish, which is then traditionally used as a dip for vegetables, meat, fish, fruit, salads, herbs and eggs. This simple recipe is a great way to get started in the world of Thai relishes. Get set up with a large granite pestle and mortar and it will be ready in no time.

Makes about 300g (10½oz). Gluten-free. Vegetarian, vegan (use seaweed sauce or soy sauce in place of shrimp paste and fish sauce)

| 1 tablespoon fermented shrimp paste | 3 banana shallots, unpeeled | 200g (7oz) banana (Turkish) chillies, stems removed | large pinch of caster sugar | 1 tablespoon tamarind paste | juice of ½ lime |

Preheat the oven to 200°C/400°F/gas mark 6.

Wrap the fermented shrimp paste in foil and roast in the oven for 10 minutes to take the edge off it. Remove and set aside.

Roast and prepare the ingredients. Put the banana shallots, **1 unpeeled head of garlic** and the banana chillies on a nonstick baking tray and roast on the middle shelf of the oven for 20–25 minutes until all the ingredients are beginning to colour and soften. Remove from the oven and set aside to cool.

Peel the garlic cloves and shallots and discard the skins, then pound to a paste with the chillies using a pestle and mortar to make a coarse paste. Add the sugar, tamarind paste, lime juice, shrimp paste and **1 teaspoon of fish sauce** and then taste. It should be salty, spicy and earthy, so adjust to suit your taste.

Serve the relish with sticky rice to dip and pork scratchings (omit if vegetarian/vegan) or cucumber for a tasty nibble.

CHILLI, GALANGAL & MINT SAUCE

This is the perfect condiment for a large roasted joint of meat or vegetables, or to be spooned over curry and rice to add a fresh kick. In my restaurant, Farang, my favourite dish to serve this with is barbecued lamb shoulder, and for vegetarians or vegans it's great spooned over roast potatoes. It is just as tasty if you use fresh ginger instead of galangal. Of course, for best results, make this fresh using a pestle and mortar, but if you are in a rush, you can pulse-blend it through a food processor.

Makes about 150ml (¼ pint). Vegetarian, vegan, gluten-free

about 20g (¾oz) galangal (or ginger), peeled and roughly chopped	2 tablespoons caster sugar	juice of 1 lime	50ml (2fl oz) white vinegar	small handful of mint leaves, chopped	small handful of coriander leaves, chopped

Using a pestle and mortar, pound the galangal to a paste, using a pinch of salt as an abrasive. Add **2 roughly chopped red or green bird's eye chillies** and continue to pound until the two ingredients are thoroughly combined, then add the caster sugar, lime juice and vinegar and stir with the pestle.

Finish the sauce with the chopped mint and coriander leaves and taste. The sauce should be a little sweet, spicy and salty with a sour, moreish edge. Bear in mind that it is a loose, fresh sauce, designed to be eaten within a week (if kept in an airtight container in the fridge), not to be mistaken for the classic, thick, British mint sauce.

TIP
Only chop the mint leaves just before serving as they go brown quickly.

TOMATO, CHILLI & TAMARIND BARBECUE SAUCE

This sauce is best made using a barbecue and was discovered by accident when we were cooking street food a few years ago. We had made a marinade for chicken and then left it in our kettle barbecue with the lid down for an hour. The residual heat and smoke from the cherry wood reduced the marinade into a wonderful, thick dipping sauce, not too dissimilar to barbecue sauce.

Makes about 500ml (18fl oz). Gluten-free. Vegetarian, vegan (use vegetable stock and seaweed sauce or soy sauce instead of fish sauce)

500g (1lb 2oz) cherry tomatoes	3 banana shallots, unpeeled	100g (3½oz) tamarind paste	150g (5½oz) palm sugar (or 75g/2¾oz caster sugar)	100ml (3½fl oz) chicken stock

Preheat a barbecue (using wood) until hot, or preheat the oven to 200°C/400°F/gas mark 6.

Put **100g (3½oz) of long red chillies**, the cherry tomatoes, **8 unpeeled garlic cloves** and the shallots in a bowl and drizzle with **3 tablespoons of vegetable oil** and a pinch of salt, rubbing them in with your hands to coat all the vegetables.

If using a barbecue, place the oiled spices and veg over the hot barbecue and cook for 15–20 minutes, turning occasionally, until they have softened and charred a little. If using an oven, spread out the oiled ingredients on a nonstick baking tray, place on the top shelf and roast for 20 minutes until all the ingredients have charred a little and softened.

Put the barbecued/roasted ingredients to one side until cool enough to handle, then peel the garlic cloves and shallots, discarding the skins.

Using a pestle and mortar or a food processor, combine the roasted vegetables, garlic and shallots with the tamarind paste, sugar, **3 tablespoons of fish sauce** and the stock to make a sauce. Pour this sauce into a heatproof tray and return to the barbecue with the lid down, or the oven, and reduce and simmer for a further 30–40 minutes until it has turned into a thick dipping sauce.

When ready, remove from the heat and set aside to cool. Have a taste, it should be sweet, salty, sour and smoky. Use the sauce as you would any other barbecue sauce for dipping, marinating or stir-frying. It keeps for up to a week in the fridge in a sterilized bottle or jar, but once opened, keep refrigerated and use within 3 days.

SWEET FISH SAUCE

There are many different brands of fish sauce available, generally the clearer the sauce the tastier, in my opinion. Gently infusing fish sauce with pineapple can take the edge off the saltiness, which can be very delicious when using the fish sauce without cooking it, in recipes for salad dressings and dipping sauces. The fructose released into the fish sauce as it infuses creates a very tasty product to use for stir-fries, too. Something to remember is that fish sauce discolours as it oxidizes, so ensure you keep your fish sauce in an airtight container in the fridge to keep it at its best for longer.

Makes 500ml (18fl oz). Gluten-free

| 500ml (18fl oz) fish sauce | 100g (3½oz) pineapple, peeled, cored and roughly chopped |

In an airtight container, mix the pineapple with the 500ml (18fl oz) of fish sauce, then store in the fridge, as simple as that. The flavour infusion will have worked overnight, however, it improves as time goes on and will keep in the fridge for up to 6 months.

THREE- OR FOUR-FLAVOURED SAUCE

I have always found the name of this sauce quite funny as it actually has four key flavours in it. Traditionally, the three refers to sweetness from the palm sugar, saltiness from the fish sauce and sourness from the tamarind. However, the title seems to forget about the spiciness added from the chillies, so I'm going to go ahead and change that for the purpose of simplicity.

Makes 400–500g (14oz–1lb 2oz) sauce. Gluten-free. Vegetarian, vegan (use seaweed sauce or soy sauce instead of fish sauce)

1 tablespoon ground white pepper	150g (5½oz) palm sugar	100g (3½oz) tamarind paste

Slice **100g (3½oz) of long red chillies** and **100g (3½oz) of long green chillies** into 1cm (½in) chunks and soak in cold water for 1 hour, then drain.

Using a pestle and mortar, pound together **8 peeled garlic cloves**, the soaked chillies and the white pepper to make a lumpy paste. Chunks are nice in this sauce, so don't worry too much about making it smooth.

Next, heat **3 tablespoons of vegetable oil** in a medium, nonstick saucepan over a medium heat, then add the chilli and garlic paste and fry, scraping it with a spatula. Continue to scrape and fry until the paste starts to turn golden brown and stick to the pan a little.

Deglaze the pan with **2–3 tablespoons of fish sauce**, scraping any ingredients that may have stuck to the pan back into the sauce. Next, add the palm sugar and gently melt this into the ingredients, creating a thick, chunky sauce. Once melted, remove from the heat, add the tamarind paste, then stir well and taste. It should be a delicious balance of sweet, salty, sour and spicy.

This sauce is a great addition to a stir-fry, or just poured over a piece of fried fish or grilled meat. It keeps indefinitely in the fridge in a sterilized bottle or jar, but once opened, keep refrigerated and use within 3 days.

STICKY PULLED PORK BELLY RELISH

This is the perfect condiment to have out at the table during a meal. Eat it with a spoon – it's delicious. Dip into it with bread, vegetables, sour fruit, crisps – it's delicious. Spread in a burger, drop it into a stir-fry, eat it with rice, to be honest, I can't think of much that it wouldn't sit next to comfortably, so give it a go.

Makes about 500g (1lb 2oz). Gluten-free (use seaweed sauce or gluten-free soy sauce)

3cm (1¼in) piece of cassia bark (or cinnamon stick)	300g (10½oz) piece of boneless pork belly (skin on)	200g (7oz) palm sugar	2 fresh bay leaves, torn to release flavour (or dried, if you like)	1 tablespoon sesame oil	50ml (2fl oz) dark soy sauce	50ml (2fl oz) oyster sauce

Lightly toast the cassia bark (or cinnamon stick) in a dry frying pan over a medium heat for 3-5 minutes, then remove to a plate and cool.

Braise the pork. Submerge the pork belly in a medium pot filled with salted water, cover with a lid and bring to a simmer. Gently simmer for 30–40 minutes, or until the pork belly is soft throughout and you can easily slide a butter knife through the whole piece. Remove the pork from the pot and set aside until cool enough to handle. Discard the cooking water.

Preheat the oven to 180°C/350°F/gas mark 4.

Remove the skin from the pork using a sharp knife and then roughly chop the belly into 3cm (1¼in) chunks and set aside. Place the skin on a baking tray and roast for 30–35 minutes until golden brown and crispy, then remove and leave to cool.

Add the sugar, toasted cassia bark (or cinnamon), bay leaves, sesame oil, soy sauce, oyster sauce and **1 tablespoon of fish sauce** to a separate pan and gently melt together to create a thick sauce. It should taste sweet, salty and rich.

Add the chopped pork belly to the sauce and stir well. Cover with a cartouche (circle of nonstick baking parchment placed directly on top of the mix) and simmer over a low heat for 1½ hours, or until the belly can easily be chopped using a spoon.

Using a large granite or wooden pestle and mortar, pound the pork crackling to a coarse powder, then reserve some of it for garnish. Add the cooked pork belly, piece by piece, pounding it with the pestle to break it into strands, like pulled pork. Finish by adding the sauce and mixing together. Serve the relish in a bowl and dust the top with the reserved pork crackling powder. Serve with sticky rice and cucumber for dipping.

GREEN SWEET CHILLI DIPPING SAUCE

Sweet chilli sauce has become a staple condiment in kitchens around the world. You can make loads of different types of sweet chilli, but this recipe is a great one to try. By using long green chillies, the sauce has a very hot and earthy flavour compared to your standard sweet chilli sauce. Remove the seeds from the large chillies in this recipe as they can add too much bitterness. The heat is added via the bird's eye chillies, so don't worry, it still has a good kick. Try to wear disposable gloves when you are deseeding this many chillies.

Makes about 500ml (18fl oz). Vegetarian, vegan (both optional), gluten-free (use gluten-free soy sauce)

| 25g (1oz) ginger, peeled and roughly chopped | 500g (18oz) caster sugar | 50ml (18fl oz) white vinegar |

It doesn't really get much simpler than this. Blitz **500g (1lb 4oz) of deseeded, roughly chopped, long green chillies**, the **peeled cloves from 1 head of garlic** and the ginger in a food processor until they form a coarse paste. Transfer this paste to a large pot with the sugar, vinegar, **100g (3½oz) of green bird's eye chillies, 100ml (3½fl oz) fish sauce** (or soy sauce), a large pinch of salt and 1 litre (1¾ pints) of water and bring to the boil over a medium heat. Stir well throughout so that the sugar melts into the mix evenly; if it settles on the bottom of the pan it may caramelize rather than melt, changing the colour and flavour.

Once boiling, reduce the heat to low and simmer until the mixture has reduced by roughly half, this should take 1–1½ hours. To check that the sauce is the desired consistency for use as a dipping sauce, place a teaspoon of the mixture on to a cold plate and tilt the plate vertically, allowing the sauce to run down it. If it runs slow and thick, then remove from the heat as the sauce is ready. If it's still a little thin, just leave it over the heat for a while longer. If it's a little over-reduced, almost to the point of jam, just loosen it up with a splash of water.

Once you are happy with the thickness of the sauce, remove from the heat and leave to cool before serving, or transfer to sterilized jars or bottles while hot and seal, then cool. This sauce will keep indefinitely in the fridge in the sealed jars/bottle, though it may slightly discolour over time but that will not have an impact on its deliciousness. Once opened, keep refrigerated and use within 3 months before it oxidizes and changes colour too much.

SPICED SWEET PLUM SAUCE

Ever since I was a kid this classic has been a strong favourite of mine. For me, nothing goes with this sauce better than duck. Try it with a whole roast duck, spring onions and some stir-fried green vegetables for a tasty treat. A delicious vegetarian or vegan option is to serve it with roasted sweet potatoes and beetroot. This sauce mixed 50/50 with my hoisin sauce (see page 152) is also delicious.

Makes about 250g (9oz). Vegetarian, vegan, gluten-free (use gluten-free soy sauce, if you like)

| ½ white onion, diced | 1 dried or fresh bay leaf, torn to release flavour | 5g (¼oz) piece of cassia bark (or cinnamon stick), toasted and ground to a powder | 750g (1lb 10oz) plums (sharp in flavour and slightly unripe are best), stoned and roughly chopped | 75ml (2¾fl oz) light soy sauce | 100g (3½fl oz) palm sugar (or 50g/1¾oz caster sugar) | 50ml (1¾fl oz) white wine vinegar (optional) |

Heat **200ml (7fl oz) of vegetable** oil in a saucepan over a medium heat, then fry **6 peeled garlic cloves (pounded to a paste or minced with a knife)**, the onion and bay leaves for 3 minutes until they turn translucent and start to brown a little at the edges. It will seem like a lot of oil, but you do need a good amount here. Next, add the cassia bark or cinnamon stick and the plums and continue to fry for a further 10–15 minutes until the plums have all broken down.

Add the soy sauce, sugar and 200ml (7fl oz) of water and simmer for a further 20 minutes, or until the plums have fully disintegrated into one lumpy mixture and all the flavours have truly got to know each other.

Remove from the heat and, using a hand-held stick blender, blitz the mixture into a smooth, silky sauce – as you do so, the oil will amalgamate into the sauce. Finally, taste the sauce. It should be sweet, sour from the plums, salty and savoury with a glossy finish from the oil. However, if your plums are ripe and sweet, add some of the white wine vinegar to balance with some sharpness.

Store the sauce in sterilized bottles or jars in the fridge and use within a month.

CAULIFLOWER KIMCHI

"Kimchi!" Not very Thai, as we all know, but with a few cheeky twists it can sit boldly next to an array of dishes, and we regularly incorporate this recipe from senior chef de partie Richard Schwe on to the menu at Farang. What is given here represents the most basic recipe that demands customization and that works best when you can get sweet, sharp and spicy flavours all at the same time. Think grated carrot or apple, finely diced red onion and a little minced garlic. You will need a large preserving jar, 1 litre (1¾ pint) capacity, sterilized by washing it in hot water, then drying it in a low oven. Leave to cool before handling it if you like your fingertips.

Makes about 400g (14oz). Gluten-free

50g (1¾oz) rice flour	30g (1oz) caster or granulated sugar	1 large cauliflower, trimmed into small florets	25g (1oz) dried chilli flakes	15g (½oz) ginger, peeled and minced

Start by gently heating 300ml (½ pint) of water, the rice flour and sugar together in a pan until a smooth slurry comes together. Use a wooden spatula to discipline the mix into its desired state, then remove from the heat and leave to cool.

Next, take your trimmed cauliflower, place it in a bowl and sprinkle over **30g (1oz) of sea salt**, ensuring everything is nicely coated. Leave this to sit for an hour, then rinse off with cold water and leave to drain in a sieve.

Mix your drained cauliflower with **2 tablespoons plus 1 teaspoon (35ml/1¼fl oz) of fish sauce** and the chilli flakes and ginger, then add this to the slurry and mix, ensuring everything is nicely incorporated.

Now take this gooey mass and place into your sterilized jar. You want a lot of clear space between the mix and the lid for reasons that will become clear later.

Finally, place the lid on loosely, leave the jar somewhere out of direct sunlight, but not too cool, for at least 24 hours, preferably 48 hours. Then secure the lid tightly and store in the fridge for up to 3 months.

So why the large jar? As your kimchi matures, gases are produced from the fermenting process that might result in a kimchi explosion when you open your jar. When the time comes, it is best to open your jar in a sink with the lid facing away from you.

PICKLED CUCUMBER & APPLE

This basic and simple pickle liquor is extremely versatile and is a great way to pickle fresh ingredients in a subtle manner. In Thailand, it is known as "ajat" and is essentially a light pickle which fresh vegetables can be glossed in to add a zing, making them perfect accompaniments to salads and curries, or simply just some nice pickles to go on the table with your meal. Other vegetables I pickle with this recipe are fennel, cabbage, pak choi and Thai shallots or onions. Have a play around and see what works for you.

Feeds 4. Vegetarian, vegan, gluten-free

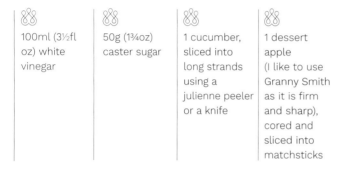

100ml (3½fl oz) white vinegar	50g (1¾oz) caster sugar	1 cucumber, sliced into long strands using a julienne peeler or a knife	1 dessert apple (I like to use Granny Smith as it is firm and sharp), cored and sliced into matchsticks

Pour 100ml (3½fl oz) of water into a deep, medium saucepan, then add the vinegar, caster sugar and a pinch of sea salt and heat over a medium heat, stirring. Once the sugar and salt have dissolved, remove from the heat and set aside to cool (add a little ice if you are in a hurry to eat the pickles).

Once cool, combine the pickle liquor, cucumber and apple in a serving dish and serve within the hour, keeping it in the fridge until ready to serve.

For added freshness, you can add some picked Thai basil leaves or dill to this arrangement of pickles – the flavour combination is awesome.

"HOISIN" SAUCE WITH FERMENTED BLACK BEANS & PRUNES

This is technically a Chinese condiment, but it has become a firm favourite in my restaurant for so long now that I had to include it here. To be honest, I love hoisin sauce so much I would actually struggle to get on with anyone who didn't like it, so perhaps put this book down and walk away if its inclusion upsets you. If you're still reading, try this sauce with some fried onions and a roast pork belly, it's phenomenal. Or, if you are vegetarian or vegan, have it with some stir-fried vegetables and rice.

Makes about 300g (10½oz). Gluten-free (use gluten-free soy sauce)

100g (3½oz) fermented black beans (more if your prefer a stronger and saltier flavour)	40g (1½oz) ginger, peeled and pounded to a paste using a pestle and mortar (or finely chopped)	4 banana shallots, diced	200g (7oz) dark soft brown sugar	3 tablespoons rice wine vinegar	6 dried prunes, pitted and chopped a little	½ teaspoon Chinese Five-spice powder

Soak the fermented black beans in warm water for about an hour, then rinse and drain.

Heat **2 tablespoons of vegetable oil** in a saucepan over a medium heat until hot, then sweat **4 peeled, finely chopped garlic cloves**, the ginger and shallots for 5 minutes until soft and translucent.

Remove from the heat and tip into a food processor or large mortar, add all the other ingredients, including the fermented black beans, plus 100ml (3½fl oz) of water and **4 tablespoons of fish sauce** and pound them together until smooth using either the pestle. Alternatively, blitz everything in a food processor. Have a taste, the sauce should be mega umami, salty, savoury, sweet and a little sour and addictively moreish. If the black beans make it too intense, add a little more water, vinegar and sugar, mix and taste again until you are happy.

Store the sauce in a sterilized jar or bottle in the fridge and use within a month.

ROASTED CHILLI "JAEW"

This is the perfect condiment to have on tap. Whether at a party for people to keep nibbling on, or placed on the family dinner table, it can be served with pork scratchings, prawn crackers or fresh vegetables, such as fennel or cucumber, to dip, or it can be dropped into stir-fries, used as a dip for grilled or fried meats, even spread on a burger. It's delicious, so go to town and enjoy.

Makes 400–500g (14oz–1lb 2oz). Vegetarian or vegan (if you exchange fish sauce for soy sauce or seaweed sauce), gluten-free (use gluten-free soy sauce, if you like)

| 4 banana shallots, unpeeled | 3 banana (Turkish) chillies | 2 lemongrass stalks | 100g (3½oz) cherry tomatoes | 2 tablespoons palm sugar (or 1 tablespoon caster sugar) | juice of 1 lime | 2 tablespoons thick tamarind paste |

Preheat the oven to 200°C/400°F/gas mark 6.

Spread out the shallots, **1 head of garlic, 6 long red chillies, 6 green bird's eye chillies,** the banana chillies, lemongrass and tomatoes on a large, nonstick baking tray and drizzle with **3 tablespoons of vegetable oil** and a pinch of salt. Place the tray on the top shelf of the oven and roast for 20 minutes, then remove all the ingredients except the lemongrass. Return this to the oven for a further 10 minutes until soft throughout. Once cooked, remove and leave with the other vegetables for a few minutes until they are cool enough to handle.

Peel the garlic and the shallots and discard the skins. Peel the tough outer layer from the lemongrass, then thinly slice the rest of the stalks.

Finally, combine and season the relish. Using either a large granite pestle and mortar or a food processor, pound or pulse-blend the shallots, garlic, lemongrass, tomatoes, sugar and chillies together to make a thick relish consistency (the residual heat from the vegetables should help to melt the sugar).

Next, add the lime juice, **2 tablespoons of fish sauce** and the tamarind paste and stir well. Have a little taste, the relish should be smoky, fresh, salty and sweet, so adjust the seasoning a little, if you like.

This relish will keep in an airtight container in the fridge for up to a week, but will likely need a re-season after being in the fridge for a day or so.

SWEET

STUFF

CUSTARD APPLE & COCONUT BAKED STICKY RICE

Custard apples need to be left to ripen for a few days out of the fridge until they become soft and sweet. If you cannot find ripe custard apples or don't want to wait, don't worry as they soften and sweeten as you cook them, so you can cheat a little.

Feeds 2-3. Vegetarian, gluten-free

100g (3½oz) Thai sticky rice	200ml (7fl oz) coconut cream	3 tablespoons caster sugar	1 heaped tablespoon rice flour	1 custard apple, peeled, deseeded and cored, diced	3 tablespoons condensed milk

First, wash the rice by putting it in a sieve and running cold water over it for 1 minute, or until the water is running clear and all the starch has been removed. Next, soak the rice, submerged in cold water, for a minimum of 2 hours, ideally overnight.

Next, set up a rice steamer. A pan half-filled with water with a colander on top can work, then once the water is boiling, clingfilm the colander to create a steamer. When the water is boiling, reduce the heat to medium, add the soaked sticky rice to the colander, cover with clingfilm and cook for 20–25 minutes. Check that the grains are soft throughout before removing from the steamer and tipping into a heatproof bowl.

Meanwhile, make the custard apple and coconut custard. Add the coconut cream, caster sugar and a big pinch of salt to a medium, nonstick saucepan, then cook over a medium heat, stirring regularly, until the cream comes to a very gentle simmer (but don't let it boil, otherwise it will split). Taste the cream, it should be sweet but a little savoury from the salt too, so adjust it slightly, if necessary. Add a ladleful of the warm coconut cream to the rice flour in a bowl and whisk into a slurry with no lumps, then add this to the remaining coconut cream with the diced custard apple and condensed milk. Continue to simmer for a further 8–10 minutes until the sauce is thick and the custard apple is soft.

Preheat the oven to 180°C/350°F/gas mark 4.

Combine the steamed rice with the coconut cream and custard apple sauce and mix thoroughly. Taste and add a little more salt or sugar as necessary. Transfer this mix to a deep 32 x 22cm (12½ x 8½in) ovenproof dish and bake for about 20 minutes. The rice should have started to go golden brown around the edges but still be soft and juicy in the middle.

Serve the baked rice warm, with a little extra custard apple scattered over the top to decorate, if you want to impress.

WATERMELON, LIME, MANGO & ORANGE ICE LOLLIES

This has to be one of the easiest recipes I have ever made; they are delicious, healthy and you can make them faster than you can drink a cup of tea, minus the freezing time, of course. This is a perfect one for the kids as it's packed full of fresh fruit and it will shut them up for a little bit if you get them to peel the fruit. Not to mention they get a tasty reward at the end. Of course you can purchase ice-lolly moulds online for this; I have a 12 x 60ml (2¼fl oz) ice-lolly moulds (never thought I would write these words), but if you want to go rogue, there are ways. Using small tumblers, place the lolly mixture in the glasses and freeze each with a teaspoon in it as a replacement for the stick. When frozen, gently warm the outside of each glass and the lolly should fall out. These will not look elegant but will work.

Makes 12 x 60ml (2¼fl oz) ice lollies. Vegetarian, vegan, gluten-free

500g (1lb 2oz) peeled fresh watermelon, seeds removed, roughly chopped	2 ripe mangoes, peeled, stoned and roughly chopped	3 large oranges, zest of 1 and juice of 3	zest and juice of 1 lime

Put all the ingredients into a blender with a small pinch of salt and blitz together until combined. Next, pour the blended mix into a measuring jug (you want 720ml/generous 1¼ pints) of the mix to make 12 ice lollies, so if it is a little short, then top up with cold water, or if it is too much, make more lollies or drink it.

To make the lollies, pour this mix into the lolly moulds and then freeze overnight. If you're too desperate to wait overnight, then start checking after about 4 hours and you should be able to eat them soon after.

Pop them out of their moulds to serve (briefly dipping the moulds into warm water if they need a helping hand).

PINEAPPLE SORBET & MERINGUES

Sorbet is a brilliant thing to make at home, just bear in mind that a good sorbet is based on the ice and sugar crystals being distributed well within the mix, so the sorbet needs to be moved regularly while it is freezing. If you like this recipe, then replace the pineapple with your favourite fruit purée to make your own.

Makes about 2 litres (3½ pints). Vegetarian, vegan (without the meringue), gluten-free

| 2 fresh pineapples, about 1kg (2lb 4oz) flesh | 800g (1lb 12oz) caster sugar | 50g (1¾oz) liquid glucose | 50g (1¾oz) icing sugar | 4 egg whites | 1 teaspoon white vinegar |

First, make the sorbet. Add the pineapple to a pan with 300ml (½ pint) of water, 750g (1lb 10oz) of the caster sugar and the liquid glucose and simmer over a medium heat for 10 minutes until the sugar has dissolved and the pineapple has started to break down. Remove from the heat and blend using a hand-held stick blender until it is as smooth as possible, then pass it through a sieve into a bowl. Set aside to cool.

Once cool, pour the mixture into a shallow, freezerproof container and put in the freezer with no lid. Remove every hour and blitz using a hand-held blender or electric whisk until too frozen to stir any more. Put the lid on and freeze for several hours or overnight.

To make the meringues, preheat the oven to 160°C/325°F/gas mark 3. Line a baking tray with nonstick baking parchment. Place the remaining 50g (1¾oz) of caster sugar and the icing sugar together on the baking tray and place in the oven. Warm for 5–6 minutes until the sugar is just starting to melt around the edges and turn to liquid.

Meanwhile, put the egg whites in a mixing bowl and beat using an electric whisk until fluffy and opaque (this is the soft peak stage where you can turn the bowl upside down and the mix will not fall out of the bowl). While whisking continuously, gently add the warm sugars, a tablespoon at a time, until all the sugar is dissolved into the mixture. Finally, add the vinegar and give it one final whisk to make sure everything is combined.

Reduce the oven temperature to 110°C/225°F/gas mark ¼. Line the baking tray with a fresh piece of nonstick baking parchment. Scoop the meringue in 1 tablespoon portions on to the lined baking tray, then place on the middle shelf and bake for about 1½ hours until the meringues are turning a light golden brown on the outside. Remove them from the oven and transfer to a wire rack (still on the paper) to cool. Once cool, carefully peel them off the paper to serve.

Serve scoops of pineapple sorbet in bowls and place the meringues over the top.

LEMONGRASS & WATERMELON GRANITA

This works well with any fresh fruit. Try serving the granita on a fruit salad made from rambutans, lychees and mangoes if you find yourself anywhere near an Asian supermarket. The sharpness of the granita is a treat balanced with sweet tropical fruit.

Makes 700ml (1¼ pints); Feeds 8–10. Vegetarian, vegan, gluten-free

| 180g (6¼oz) caster sugar | 4 kaffir lime leaves, torn to release their flavour | 6 lemongrass stalks, tough outer layer removed, bruised using a pestle and mortar | 500g (1lb 2oz) watermelon flesh (peeled, deseeded weight), blitzed to a purée, plus an extra few large slices for grilling | 150ml (¼ pint) soda water | 350ml (12fl oz) fresh lime juice |

Pour 180ml (6¼fl oz) of water into a large pan, add the caster sugar, a pinch of salt, the kaffir lime leaves and lemongrass and heat over a medium heat for 8–10 minutes until the sugar has dissolved and the flavours have fused. Remove from the heat and leave for a few hours at room temperature to allow the lemongrass to infuse into the syrup. Once infused, remove and discard the lime leaves and lemongrass, then stir in the watermelon purée, mixing well.

Add the soda water and lime juice to the watermelon mix and stir gently. Try not to stir all the bubbles out of the soda water as this is the reason for using it. Pour into a shallow, freezerproof container, cover with a lid and transfer to the freezer. Take it out every couple of hours and, using a fork, scrape the granita so that you end up with fluffy ice, rather than one big block of ice. It should take 4–6 hours to freeze.

To serve, heat a griddle pan over a high heat until hot, then cook the watermelon slices for 2 minutes on each side – the natural sugars will begin to caramelize and you should get some tasty grill lines appearing.

Scoop portions of the granita into bowls, top with the grilled watermelon slices and sprinkle the watermelon with a small pinch of sea salt.

BANANA & MAPLE JAM ROTI

You can now find an endless array of delicious fillings and coatings for roti, both sweet and savoury. Traditionally roti bread contains condensed milk and eggs, but exchange these for olive oil and the result is a delicious, light, flaky flatbread. Roti bread was introduced to Thai culture by Indonesian immigrants, and being a cheap, easy and affordable snack, the roti became a reliable form of income for those with little funds who had to make their living on the streets. Banana roti is a staple street food snack found across Thailand. This is my version and if you want to start the day right, it makes for a banging breakfast. The dough keeps in the fridge for at least a week so it can be pre-prepped for ease on those lazy mornings.

Feeds 4. Vegetarian, vegan

| 700g (1lb 9oz) plain flour, plus extra for dusting | 50ml (2fl oz) olive oil | 4 bananas | 100g (3½fl oz) light soft brown sugar, plus extra for serving | 50ml (2fl oz) maple syrup | 2cm (¾in) piece of cassia bark (or cinnamon stick) | 1 lime, sliced into cheeks or wedges |

First, make the roti dough. Sift the flour and a pinch of salt into a mixing bowl and make a well in the middle. Add the olive oil to the well and, using a fork, begin stirring the oil into the flour until it starts to resemble breadcrumbs. Then, little by little, add 350ml (12fl oz) of warm water and continue stirring until the mix comes together in a ball of dough. Now get stuck in with your hands and knead for 4–5 minutes, adding a little extra flour if the dough is still tacky. Cover your hands and the worktop with flour – basically, if you're not covered in flour, you're not doing it right. Once kneaded, the dough should not be sticky and it should be soft to the touch. This dough is quite loose and if you push your finger into the dough, it will remain indented.

Place the dough in a lightly oiled bowl, then cover with clingfilm, ensuring the clingfilm is in direct contact with the dough to stop it crusting over. Leave to rest for a minimum of 30 minutes, a maximum of 4 hours, at room temperature. This dough can be stored in the fridge for up to 1 week, but bring it back to room temperature slowly before using.

Meanwhile, make the banana jam. Peel and roughly chop the bananas, then place in a medium saucepan with the brown sugar, maple syrup, cassia bark or cinnamon stick and 4–6 teaspoons of water. Cook over a medium heat for 20–30 minutes, stirring regularly, until the bananas have broken down and the mixture has come together with the sugar beginning to darken and caramelize. Finish with a pinch of salt and then remove from the heat. This is delicious eaten hot with roti or it can be stored in a sterilized jar for up to 3 months in the fridge and used like any other fruit jam. Discard the cassia bark or cinnamon stick before serving/storing. ⟶

Now for the fun bit, cooking the roti. If you're feeling lucky, then try the traditional method by slapping out the roti dough. Lightly oil a clean surface. Divide the dough into 4–6 even portions and form each into a small ball (about the size of a golf ball).

Next, place a dough ball on the oiled surface. Flatten it into a rough circle and gently lift the side closest to you and drag it towards you, then lift it quickly but delicately and slap it back on the surface (the elasticity and stickiness of the dough means that it doesn't rip too easily and it stretches bigger as you drag it). Repeat this process until the dough is roughly 2–3mm (⅟₁₆–⅛in) thick (the thinner the better, and a few holes are fine). Alternatively, you can use a rolling pin, or just stretch it out with your hands. It's hard to get it perfect the first time, so don't worry if it all goes a little pear-shaped, it will still taste amazing. Repeat with the remaining balls of dough.

Heat **1 tablespoon of vegetable oil** in a large frying pan over a medium heat (the oil needs to be really hot in order to crisp the dough, but not burn it). Delicately lift a piece of dough into the pan; if it sizzles you're doing it right. As soon as the dough starts to cook, place a good few tablespoons of banana jam in the centre. Fold the sides of the dough over into a rectangle shape and then flip over. Fry for roughly 2 minutes on each side until it is golden brown and crispy on both sides. Remove to a resting tray lined with kitchen paper to drain off any excess oil, while you cook and assemble the remaining rotis in the same way.

Serve the rotis straight away. For tasty results, finish with a little sprinkle of light soft brown sugar and a good squeeze of lime. This is a perfect snack and can be eaten at any point in the day.

BAKED TAMARIND, PEANUTS, MANDARIN & DARK CHOCOLATE BANANAS

This is one of those creations that came from the heart. It is in no way traditionally Thai, it is in no way traditionally British, but it's delicious and that's all that matters to me when eating.

Feeds 2. Vegetarian, optional vegan and gluten-free (if using vegan/gluten-free chocolate)

| 4 mandarins, peeled, pith removed and separated into segments | 60g (2¼oz) palm sugar (or light soft brown sugar) | 2 bananas, skin on | 80g (2¾oz) good-quality dark chocolate, roughly cut/ broken into 1cm (½in) pieces | 2 tablespoons tamarind paste | 20g (¾oz) roasted peanuts, crushed a little using a pestle and mortar (or roughly chopped) | juice of ½ lime |

First, make the mandarin jam. Put the mandarin segments in a medium pan with the sugar and a couple of tablespoons of water, then heat gently over a low heat for 45 minutes, stirring occasionally, until the mixture has turned into a thick jam. Test to see if it is ready by placing a teaspoon of jam on to a cold plate and tilting the plate sideways to see how fast the mixture runs down the plate; if it resembles a jam, then you're on, so set it aside for now.

Preheat the oven to 200°C/400°F/gas mark 6.

Using a small knife, carefully make an incision into the bananas from 1cm (½in) in from the top to 1cm (½in) up from the bottom. Do this carefully and ensure not to slice all the way through the banana, you essentially want to make a pocket within the banana to stuff with goodies. Once the pockets have been sliced, stuff the bananas with equal amounts of dark chocolate and tamarind paste and 1 tablespoon of the mandarin jam in each, then wrap the bananas individually in foil.

Place the bananas on a small baking tray and roast for 15 minutes until each banana has softened and the stuffing has melted into it. If the bananas are still hard within, then return to the oven and roast for further 5-minute intervals until ready.

Carefully remove the foil from each banana and place on a plate, they should naturally fold open showing the melted deliciousness within. Top each with a drizzle more of mandarin jam, the roasted peanuts and a squeeze of lime juice and then serve with a spoon. They should taste sweet and sour with a crunch from the peanuts. Any leftover jam can be stored in the fridge for up to a week.

APPLE & CASSIA BARK COOKIES

Cassia bark can be purchased online or in any good Asian supermarket and is well worth a try. Due to its hardy nature, it will need to be snapped into small pieces, toasted lightly in a dry pan and then ground using a spice grinder or a pestle and mortar to make it into a usable powder – or you can just buy it powdered.

Makes about 12 cookies. Vegetarian, vegan

4 large dessert or cooking apples, peeled, cored and finely diced	300g (10½oz) caster sugar	375g (13oz) plain flour, sifted	1½ teaspoons baking powder	1 teaspoon bicarbonate of soda	2 teaspoons ground cassia bark (or ground cinnamon)

Preheat the oven to 160°C/325°F/gas mark 3. Line two baking sheets with nonstick baking parchment.

Make an apple sauce by combining three of the diced apples, 2 tablespoons of water and 50g (1¾oz) of the caster sugar in a nonstick saucepan. Cook over a medium heat for about 15 minutes, stirring occasionally with a wooden spoon. The apples will break down naturally. Once it looks like a sauce with minimal chunks, remove from the heat and set aside to cool.

Meanwhile, in a large mixing bowl, whisk together the flour, baking powder, bicarbonate of soda, ground cassia bark (or cinnamon) and ¼ teaspoon of salt.

In a separate bowl, whisk together **80ml (3fl oz) of vegetable oil** (or butter) with the apple sauce, then whisk in 150g (5½oz) of the sugar. Gently fold the flour mixture into the wet mixture using a spatula, and finish by folding in the remaining diced apple.

Place the remaining 100g (3½oz) of sugar in a clean bowl. Using both your hands, roll a 50–60g (1¾–2¼oz) portion (about a heaped tablespoon) of the dough into a ball, then roll the ball in the sugar until it is completely coated and dry to the touch. Place on one of the prepared baking sheets. Repeat with the remaining dough, leaving plenty of space around the dough balls to allow room for them to expand as they cook.

Place the baking sheets on the middle shelf and bake for 20–25 minutes, or until the tops of the cookies are dry and the bottoms are golden brown. Remove from the oven and transfer to a wire rack to cool. Consume within 3 days; they are delicious eaten warm, too.

CONDENSED MILK & STEM GALANGAL BILLIONAIRE'S SHORTBREAD

I created this recipe to go with ice cream at Farang, but it's very tasty in its own right. The inclusion of stem galangal and condensed milk has taken it from millionaire to billionaire status. Stem ginger will work as a delicious substitute for the stem galagal.

Makes 20 slices. Vegetarian

50g (1¾oz) galangal, peeled and chopped into 1cm (½in) cubes	400g (14oz) light soft brown sugar	250g (9oz) plain flour, sifted	270g (9¾oz) salted butter, at room temperature	50g (1¾oz) desiccated coconut	3 x 395g (14oz) cans sweetened condensed milk	300g (10½oz) good-quality dark chocolate, chopped into small pieces

First, make the stem galangal. Put the galangal, 500ml (18fl oz) of water and 200g (7oz) of the sugar in a saucepan and bring to the boil. Reduce the heat and simmer for 1¼–1½ hours, stirring now and again, until all the liquid has reduced into a thick syrup and the galangal has softened. Remove from the heat and set aside. The stem galangal can be transferred to sterilized jars at this stage and will keep indefinitely.

Preheat the oven to 170°C/340°F/gas mark 3½. Grease a 20 x 30cm (8 x 12in) baking tray and line with nonstick baking parchment.

In a bowl, mix together the flour, 100g (3½oz) of the remaining sugar, 150g (5½oz) of the butter, the desiccated coconut and the drained galangal (reserve the syrup) until well combined. Press the mixture evenly into the base of the prepared baking tray. Bake on the middle shelf for 25 minutes until golden brown. Remove from the oven and set aside to cool in the tray for 10 minutes.

Put the condensed milk and the remaining sugar and butter in a saucepan and heat over a medium-low heat for 25–30 minutes, stirring regularly, until the mixture is smooth and starting to darken caramelize. Pour over the base in the tray and bake for 30–35 minutes, or until dark golden. Remove from the oven and set aside to cool completely in the tray.

Place the chocolate in a heatproof bowl set over a saucepan of gently simmering water. Heat for 6–8 minutes, stirring every now and then, until smooth. Once melted, cool slightly, then pour over the caramel, using a spoon to ensure that the chocolate covers the caramel completely. Chill in the fridge for 2 hours, or until set.

Once set, cut into 20 generous slices. Remove from the tray and decorate each with a drizzle of the reserved stem galangal syrup. Enjoy on their own, or serve with fresh fruit.

BANANA JAM, FRESH STRAWBERRIES & SALTED PEANUT PRALINE

This dish is also known as "the Farang mess" and was developed in the restaurant through an obsession to make the perfect meringue. After many experiments, this vegan version is one of our favourites as we replace the crunchy meringue with praline.

Feeds 2 (plus a little spare jam for breakfast). Vegetarian, vegan, gluten-free

400g (14oz) caster sugar	10g (¼oz) peanuts, toasted and semi-pounded, plus extra to serve	500g (1lb 2oz) ripe bananas, peeled and chopped into chunks	2 dessert apples, peeled, cored and chopped	40g (1½oz) strawberries, chopped	100ml (3½fl oz) coconut cream

First, make the peanut praline. Line a baking tray with nonstick baking parchment. Place 100g (3½oz) of the sugar in a heavy-based pan and melt over a medium heat, stirring constantly to ensure that it doesn't stick to the pan. Once melted, increase the heat and stir constantly until the mixture begins to darken and caramelize (6–8 minutes, once boiling). Pour the caramel on to the lined baking tray, then lift the tray and tilt it to the side to spread the mixture as thinly as possible. Sprinkle with the crushed peanuts and a pinch of sea salt, then set aside to cool and harden. Once solid, hit it with a rolling pin to break it up into portion-sized pieces and then store in an airtight container.

You will find it much easier to make this jam with a sugar thermometer, but if you don't have one, not to worry, you'll just have to keep a close eye out. First, put the bananas, apples and the remaining 300g (10½oz) of sugar in a heavy-based, nonstick pan with 50ml (2fl oz) of water and cook over a medium heat for 35–40 minutes, or until the bananas have broken down and begun to darken slightly – keep the mixture moving from time to time, otherwise it will stick. Boil until it reaches a temperature of 104–105.5°C (219–221°F), jam setting temperature; if you are not using a thermometer, then look for when the bubbles get larger and the mixture thicker. You can test the jam by putting a teaspoon of jam on to a chilled plate and seeing how it moves once cold: if it resembles jam and does not move around the plate once cool, then bingo. Once it's ready, pour the jam straight into sterilized jam jars, then seal with the lid(s) and set aside to cool. The banana jam is great used as you would any normal fruit jam and keeps indefinitely in the fridge. Once opened, keep refrigerated and use within 3 months.

To serve, place a few small spoonfuls of the jam into each bowl with some chopped strawberries and then top with a few pieces of praline. Spoon over a little coconut cream and, Iif you like, sprinkle over a few extra peanuts, too.

INDEX

THANK YOUS

This goes out to my grandad Mr Vincent Lindsey. This book would have been another for him to add to his collection of grandson memorabilia growing dust under his bed.

Also, I would like to thank the team at Farang for keeping the restaurant flowing smoothly whilst I was writing the book and the many people who contributed recipes.

Lastly, thanks to my family and friends who constantly support my endeavours and allow me to be the idiot I was born to be.